# STOLEN GIRLS

**Also by Wolfgang Bauer**

*Crossing the Sea: With Syrians on the Exodus to Europe*

# STOLEN GIRLS

## SURVIVORS OF BOKO HARAM
## TELL THEIR STORY

Wolfgang Bauer

Photographs by Andy Spyra

Translated by Eric Trump

THE NEW PRESS

25 YEARS

NEW YORK
LONDON

Requests for permission to reproduce selections from this book should be mailed to:
Permissions Department,
The New Press, 120 Wall Street, 31st floor, New York, NY 10005.

Originally published in Germany as *Die geraubten Mädchen: Boko Haram und der Terror im
Herzen Afrikas* in 2016 by Suhrkamp Verlag Berlin

Published in the United States by The New Press, New York, 2017
Distributed by Perseus Distribution

ISBN 978-1-62097-257-1 (hc)
ISBN 978-1-62097-258-8 (e-book)
CIP data is available

The New Press publishes books that promote and enrich public discussion and
understanding of the issues vital to our democracy and to a more equitable world. These
books are made possible by the enthusiasm of our readers; the support of a committed group
of donors, large and small; the collaboration of our many partners in the independent media
and the not-for-profit sector; booksellers, who often hand-sell New Press books; librarians;
and above all by our authors.

www.thenewpress.com

This book was set in Nosta and Myriad

Printed in the United States of America

2 4 6 8 10 9 7 5 3 1

# CONTENTS

*"I become through the Thou. As I become I, I say Thou."*
—Martin Buber

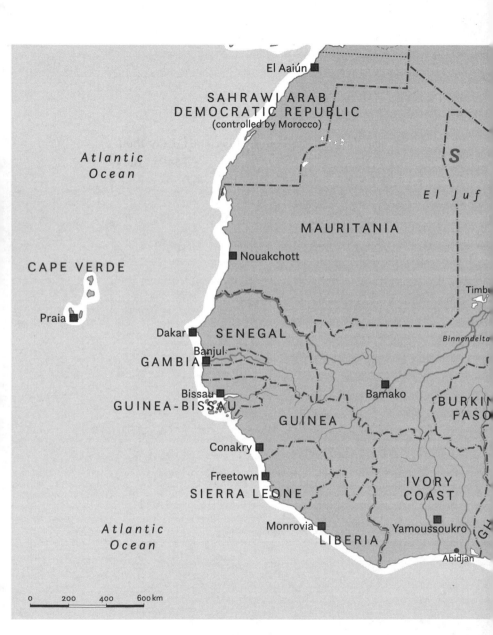

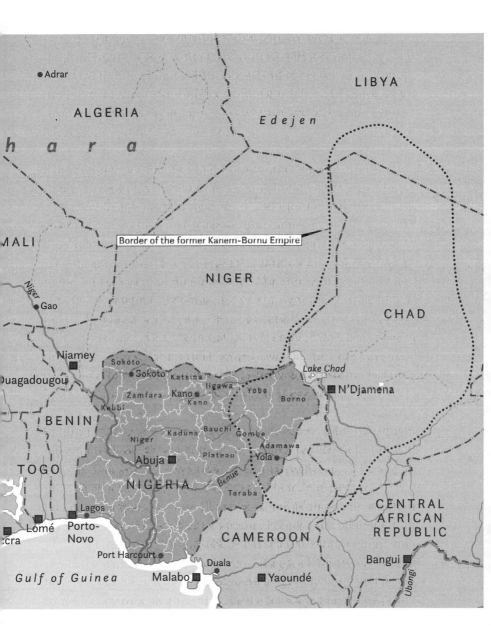

NIGER

Nguigmi

*former boundary of Lake Chad*

CHAD

Kanem

Lac

Bol

Lake Chad

Monguno

Jigawa

*Komadugu Yobe*

Jakusko

Yobe

Borno

N'Djamena

Kano

*Bunga*

*Komadugu Gana*

Damaturu

Maiduguri

A3

Kano

Bama

A4

*Sambisa-Wald*

Bitta   (capital of Boko
Haram territory)

Bauchi

*Gongola*

Gombe

Gulani

Chibok

Gwoza

Gublai   Madagali

Gulak

Pallam   SUKUR

Bauchi

Gombe

Michika

*Mandara Mountains*

NIGERIA

Mubi

Adamawa

A13

CHAD

Plateau

*Benue*

Yola

Jalingo

*Atlantika Mountains*

CAMEROON

Taraba

Sambisa Forest

The extent of Boko Haram
territory, mid-November 2014

0    50    100    150 km

The forest that became the symbol of terror in Nigeria is dark and nearly impenetrable. Those who enter never find their way out again. It is said an ancient curse lies upon it. The forest is so old that no one can say anymore what its name originally meant. The Sambisa Forest is the last of its kind. Of all the great forests in northeastern Nigeria only the Sambisa has remained. Its trees do not inspire awe; they are only a few meters high, gnarled and intertwined. The underbrush is full of thorns as sharp as claws. The forest's canopy blocks the sky. The sun rarely filters down to its most interior spaces. The ground here does not offer a firm footing. Great rivers, with sources in the Mandara Mountains, flow not to the sea, but to the Sambisa's swamps. Many predators inhabit the forest. The most dangerous of these are human beings. More precisely: men.

The highway that skirts the Sambisa is officially called A13. Gray craggy rock pillars tower over it, the remains of ancient volcanoes. The highway initially brought progress to northeastern Nigeria. It was finished at the beginning of the 1980s and was the first road to open the region to modern commerce. Its two lanes unspool from Yola, in east Nigeria, heading over 350 kilometers north, to near Bama in the northeast. Its asphalt seems to attract people irresistibly, like iron filings to a magnet. Villages, brick houses, and round mud huts crowd along the highway's route. In the past few years, settlements along it have grown ever bigger. They are called Michika, Duhu, Gulak, and Gubla. The road has until recently been a gateway for new ideas. It brought doctors, medicines, and teachers to the people living along its route. Now this same road brings them suffering and sorrow.

Sadiya, 38, market woman, mother of five, was held hostage by Boko Haram for nine months in the Sambisa Forest. She was forced to marry and, at the time of the interview, was expecting a child from the man who tormented her.

Talatu, 14, Sadiya's daughter, was in the ninth grade at the time of her abduction. She was abducted with her mother and was also forced to marry.

Batula, 41, is the elder sister of Sadiya. Market woman, mother of nine, she was a hostage for nine months in the Sambisa. At the time of her abduction, she was pregnant with her youngest child.

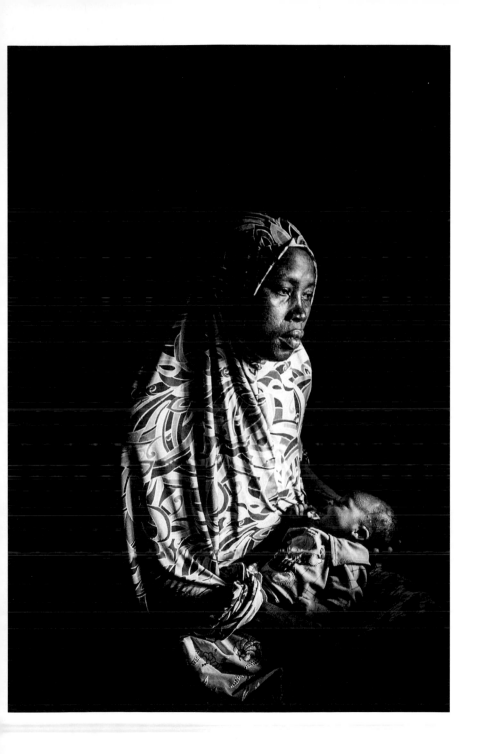

Rabi, 13, the daughter of Batula, was in the fifth grade at the time of her abduction. She was abducted with her mother and forced to marry.

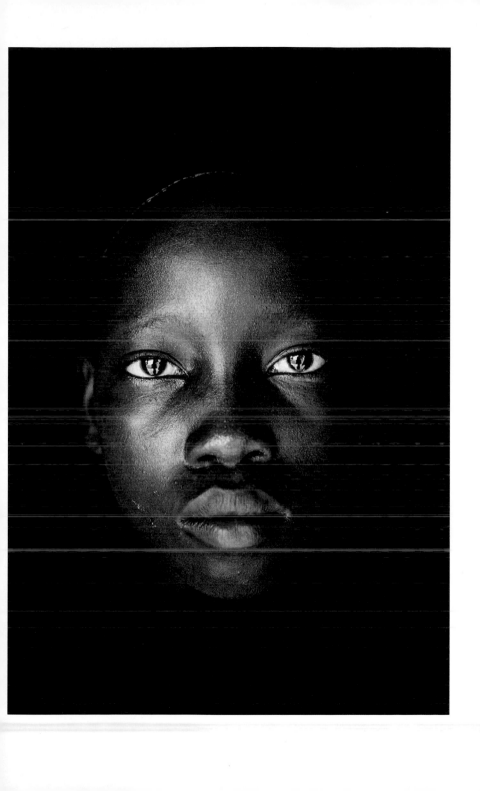

Sakinah, 33, is a midwife. Mother of six, she hid for several weeks in the mountains and was held hostage for two months. Her eldest daughter, eleven years old, died when separated from her mother while fleeing Boko Haram.

Isa, 23, a goat trader, is the cousin of Sakinah. He fled with Sakinah's husband into the mountains and hid there for several months. During their flight, they buried Sakinah's eldest daughter.

Rachel, 21, is the half sister of Sakinah. She is a farmer and was held hostage for several weeks by Boko Haram.

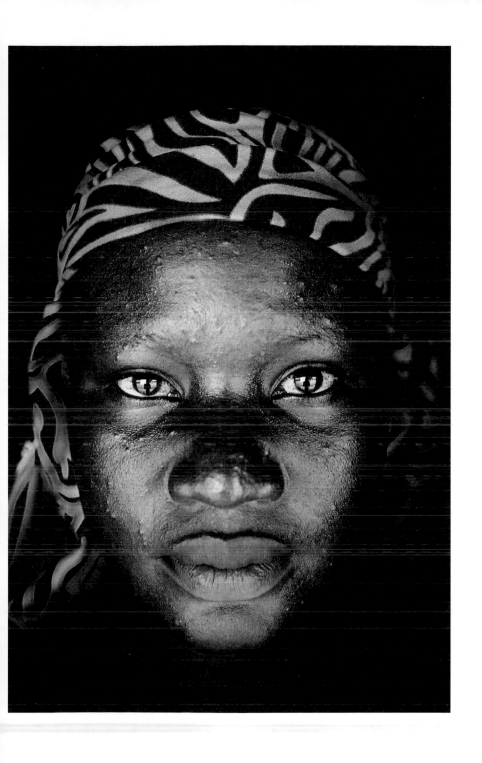

Previous two pages: Gajar, 16, is a field worker who was held hostage for seven months. She was forced to marry and give birth to her tormentor's son, Isa.

# STOLEN GIRLS

"Glory to God, our name is Jamā'at Ahl as-Sunnah lid-Da'wah wa'l-Jihād. They call us Boko Haram. Glory to God, we have given up explanations; we have said everything that needs to be said. . . .

"Some people go so far as to say that we are a cancer, which is an idiotic illness. No, we are not a cancer, and we are not an illness, and we are not capricious people with evil intentions. Even if the general public does not know us, Allah knows everyone."

—Abubakar Shekau, April 2011

# THE FOREST

**Talatu:** My name is Jummai, but everyone calls me Talatu because I was born first. Before they carried me off into the forest, I was in the high school in Duhu, in the ninth grade. My favorite subject is math. I like math because it's logical. Once you've understood the logic of a mathematical rule, you can solve every task easily and quickly.

Hidden in the swamps of the Sambisa Forest are the headquarters of terrorists who in their cruelty seem almost without comparison. They are as modern as they are archaic. The world refers to them as "Boko Haram," meaning "Western education is forbidden." They call themselves "Jamā'at Ahl as-Sunnah lid-Da'wah wa'l-Jihād," meaning "Group of the People of Sunnah for the Preaching of Islam and Jihad." They are fighting for the foundation of a caliphate in Nigeria, cooperating with al-Qaida in Mali and Algeria. By now, they have sworn allegiance to the so-called Islamic State (ISIS) in Iraq and Syria. In the summer of 2014, Boko Haram occupied a fifth of Nigeria in just a few months.

**Sadiya:** You enter the forest, and it gets dark. So dark that you forget it's still daytime. I'm the mother of Talatu. They took us both into the forest. The driver of our truck had to turn on the headlights because suddenly it was so dark.

In the West, little notice was paid to the terror that was unfolding in Nigeria—not until what happened the night of April 14, 2014. A Boko Haram commando kidnapped 276 schoolgirls from a boarding school in the small town of Chibok. They forced them into trucks and drove them into the forest from which, at the time of this writing, they have not escaped or been freed. With the abduction of the Chibok girls, the brutality of Boko Haram made international headlines. Suddenly prominent people such as Michelle Obama, the wife of the American president Barack Obama, demanded "Bring Back Our Girls." The attack on Chibok gave the intangible a name.

It is estimated that by now many thousands of women are captives of Boko Haram. Most are assumed to be held in the Sambisa and its swamps. African and European heads of state organized crisis summits to discuss the rescue of the girls. Angela Merkel, Germany's chancellor, pledged to support a West African strike force. However, the shock of Boko Haram didn't last for long. Northeastern Nigeria is far from the world's political centers of power.

In July 2015 and then again in January 2016, I interviewed more than sixty girls and women who had managed to escape from the Boko Haram slave camps. I was accompanied by a photographer and translator. Many women with whom we spoke had just escaped the forest days before. Their narratives shed light on unimaginable crimes and gave a glimpse into the inner workings of a terrorist organization that in the past few years has killed even more people than ISIS. As deadly as Boko Haram is, very little is known about it. It is unclear how it is administered, what its long-term goals are, who finances it, and how it comes to some of its decisions. The interviews with these women do not answer these questions, but they do help us to come a little closer to answering them. Their stories represent not just sources of information about Boko Haram. They are also testimonies about the women. They take us into their lives, which, despite the Internet and the effects of globalization, remain alien to us. They take us along the alleys of villages whose names we often cannot pronounce and that are marked on only a few maps. Their stories are painful, in part because they show us how limited our own perspectives still are, how straitened our awareness, and how meager our understanding of the world and the era that we call "our own."

In seemingly distant Europe and America, the catastrophe that is Boko Haram has not affected us directly so far. Most observers of the situation, however, agree that this group will one day carry out attacks in the West.

We cannot ignore Boko Haram's terror. If we refuse to look at the blood spilled by others, we will soon be looking at our own blood. We can begin to confront these terrorists successfully only when we listen to their victims: the women.

**Sadiya:** They left me only my name. They took everything else. I am now someone else. I feel that. I am now someone I do not know. I grew up in the village of Duhu in the state of Adamawa. Most of the people there are Christians, but we are Muslims. I never went to school. I had to work the fields with my mother. My father was a mason and was always on the go. When he was home, my parents argued all the time. They eventually got divorced. Then I lived with my mother.

I was happier as a child than I am today. I wanted for nothing. I miss those easy days. I was married at sixteen. He was eighteen, very handsome (*she laughs and looks at the ground*). He always played jokes. He was a truck driver and employed at a transport firm in Maiduguri, the capital of the state of Borno. He was in Duhu when his truck had a flat tire. That is how we met. I was standing with friends at a well when he came up to me. "I have never seen you here!" he said to me, smiling. That's how it started. We were married twelve years. We moved to Maiduguri and lived on the company grounds of the transport firm. We leased a small store. I sold soap, Maggi bouillon cubes, and ketchup. I hired two girls to work as sales assistants. We made a good life for ourselves. He traveled throughout the whole country, all the way to Port Harcourt in the South. Then his truck ended up in a river and he died. That was seven years ago.

The room where we meet thirty-eight-year-old Sadiya and her fourteen-year-old daughter Talatu for the first time is in a small residential building in central Yola, the capital of the Nigerian state of Adamawa. It is mid-July 2015. Both mother and daughter were abducted from their village at the end of August 2014. In June 2015, they fled their captors. We are lying on a rug because Sadiya and Talatu are uncomfortable on the sofas and chairs in the room. Where they come from, only dignitaries sit in chairs. The windows are covered with dark cloth. Outside it is brutally hot.

Yola is the last safe outpost before Boko Haram's influence begins. About 340,000 people are said to have lived here in 2010. Yola sprawls out into the surrounding lands, new neighborhoods growing like shrub and grassland. Desperate fugitives come here seeking sanctuary and stability. The encroachment of Boko Haram transformed Yola into a city of more than a million within a few months. From the air, Yola looks provincial. The houses are low to the ground, many still made of brick earth, usually one story, with corrugated tin roofs of blue, red, and yellow. Situated among the houses are open areas where the big markets set up. These are the targets time and again of bombings. High walls surround the university and administrative buildings. Only the main transportation axes are asphalted. Dust covers everything. Dust is on the yellow, three-wheeled motorbikes that are the inexpensive means of transport for most people. It covers the fleet of used European automobiles that plague the city streets.

A few hundred kilometers to the north is where the Sahel—the semi-arid southern border of the Sahara Desert—begins. This region often sends its sandstorms over Yola. When that happens, the Saharan sands darken the sun and taint the air, first a gleaming yellow, then orange, then a dim brown. The sky seems to drape itself over the city. Houses are hurriedly built, wall to wall, and are rarely ever finished because people have usually already moved in when the buildings are just bare masonry and carpentry. People exploit the refugees. The rents are exorbitant. More and more prostitutes are found in this city, where there are many churches and even more mosques. Refugees fill just about every free space between houses, every seam. Whoever can't cling to an existence in Yola—in one of the large encampments or in the house of a friend—because money runs out is forced to return to live in one of the outlying villages. Where terror still reigns. The women and girls with whom we speak come from these villages.

They have returned from a world that journalists are not able to enter. We speak over the course of two days with mother and daughter, both self-assured women. Both were kidnapped by Boko Haram. Sadiya is six months pregnant. Her belly bulges noticeably. The father of the child she carries is the man who raped her. Sadiya is tall, haggard, and fragile. Her voice is deep and raw. When she tells her story, she seems to look enraptured. Her eyes often have no expression. It is Ramadan, the Muslim month of fasting. Sadiya is a disciplined observer of the holy month, drinking nothing, praying at the prescribed times. Talatu is not. As if she is trying to provoke her mother, she drinks long and pleasurably, her mother looking away, seemingly hurt by her daughter's behavior.

Confidential intermediaries arranged our meetings with the women. After their escape from Boko Haram, they returned to their villages. Most of the women with whom we speak are Margi, a small tribe of 250,000 people. We have changed their names in order to protect them, and every day we changed the location where we met them for even in Yola Boko Haram kidnaps ever more people. The most recent attack, on a market, killed forty-five people, just two weeks before our arrival.

When we first meet the women there is much mistrust. We are afraid of them because Boko Haram has been known to force kidnapped girls to become suicide bombers. Almost daily, young women carry out suicide attacks in busy places, most because they were forced to do so. However, others do it out of conviction. Who can measure how much someone will change during a

months-long imprisonment, how much the psyche has to adjust
to survive? And of course the women we meet are afraid of us
because at first they cannot tell if we are for or against Boko
Haram. For a long time now, they have inhabited a world dominated by Boko Haram.

**Sadiya:** My husband was called Moussa. After his accident in the
truck, he was taken to the hospital, a friend told me. But that's
where he died, and I had to give up the store. The store alone
did not feed us. We needed his salary. I took inventory of what
was left in the store and returned to Duhu. My husband and I had
given the store a special name, but I have forgotten it. Strange,
isn't it? I have forgotten the name.

She concentrates and tries to think of the name for a while, falling
quiet. Then she shakes her head.

**Sadiya:** But what was I supposed to do? With all my children . . .
I did not know for a long time. I asked the two girls, whom I had
hired, to stay in the store until all the goods were sold. They sent
the money to me in Duhu. After five months, everything had
been sold. I was desperate. I had never gone to school and had
not worked the land since my marriage. I tried it again, but it was
too difficult for me. My back, it quickly began to hurt, and I had to
stop. When you do that kind of work from an early age, your body
gets used to it. But I wasn't used to it anymore. So I started cooking kosai, bean cakes fried in palm oil. I obtained a permit from
the village chief and set up a stand at the bus stop.

She coughs and spits white froth. Her chest burns. She has a
headache. She continually puts a hand to her forehead.

**Sadiya:** Talatu and I were a team at the kosai stand. She packed
the kosai cakes into plastic bags for customers and took their

money, while I fried new kosai. I always had twelve liters of oil in the giant pan. It is not easy to make kosai. You must be experienced at it. You must know exactly how much of something you must put in and when.

I get up every day at six-thirty and wash my children, put on their school uniforms, give them some money—fifty naira (*about twenty cents*)—for a snack. Talatu gets a hundred naira so she can take the bus to school. My little ones are named Estha, who's twelve, and Buba, a boy, who's ten. I give Buba a soccer ball when he goes to school so he can play with his friends during break. I give Estha knitting things to take along because she likes to knit with her friends.

When the children are in school, I go out to the fields to collect firewood for cooking. I need at least an hour to do this. The work is hard, but I like it. You have peace and quiet when you are out there. You don't have to speak a lot. You can think about everything. Then I carry the wood home on my head. I cook jollof rice with onions and tomatoes and potatoes. After cooking, I lie down for an hour until about two o'clock in the afternoon, when the children come home. They wake me, we eat, and then we leave for the bus stop. I take the giant black skillet with me. Until eleven o'clock at night Talatu and I sell kosai. I earn the most in December because of the many Christians in the village. In the evenings, I drink a jug of milk to wash down the grime left in my throat from the fire. Then I lie down again.

Boko Haram feeds off a part of Nigeria that is among the poorest in the world. Around Lake Chad, whose shores border Niger, Chad, Cameroon, and Nigeria, the majority of the people live, according to the World Bank, on no more than a dollar a day. Nigeria, located between the Sahel and the Atlantic Ocean, is in the grip of powerful forces that are threatening to tear it apart. Here, the Muslims of North Africa and the Christians of the South clash with one another. Few of the world's countries contain such contradictions as Nigeria. It is a conglomeration of 514 ethnic groups and 190 million inhabitants.

The North is a religious tectonic zone. In perhaps no other region on Earth is the force of religion so palpable as here. This is a zone of constant upheaval. Old values are dissolving. Tribes, though still very important, have lost some of their cohesive force. With the introduction of artificial fertilizers the population has grown rapidly. The changes in Nigeria are pulling North and South Nigeria further and further apart. The coastal region between the port cities of Lagos and Port Harcourt is the country's economic motor. The oil industry is located here, as well as Nigeria's legendary film industry, Nollywood, which produces more films than India's Bollywood. The wealth that southern Nigeria generates is the reason why its economy is said to have surpassed South Africa's in 2014.[1] The South of Nigeria has a significant middle class, whose collective gaze is directed at North America.

While Nigeria's South is lush and tropical, the North is predominantly sparse. Broad grasslands with solitary acacia trees cover this region. The North has few factories and most of the ones it had have shut down in the past few years. The people here live for the most part from what they cultivate themselves. However, climate change has resulted in an ever shorter rainy season, making harvests more meager than before. The cattle herds that live off the grassland have grown smaller. The North has hardly any infrastructure. According to Human Rights Watch, only 24 percent of households have access to electricity, compared with 71 percent in the southwest.[2] The people of the North are completely cut off from the economic successes of the South. Northern Nigeria orients itself not toward North America but toward Saudi Arabia and the Sudan.

When British colonists dominated Nigeria, they at first administered two separate colonies, the Southern Nigerian Protectorate and the Northern Nigerian Protectorate. The British were all too familiar with the differences between the two. After Nigerian independence was won in 1960, generals ruled the country for a long time, but since 1998 the country has been considered a democracy. The oil wells in the South have produced much wealth, but even more corruption. Nigeria's politicians have stolen billions from the state coffers. In the northeastern provinces, Boko Haram territory, the Nigerian state, insofar as it is even a presence, is above all perceived as predatory. Nigeria has the highest percentage internationally of children not attending school, with the highest rate in Nigeria being, once again, in the northeast. Seventy percent of the people are not able to read or write.[3] Despite its robust economic growth, the average life expectancy in Nigeria is just fifty-two years, nineteen fewer than the global average.[4] The differences between Nigeria and the rest of the world grow ever larger. In 2010, 61 percent of the population (115 million people) lived in absolute poverty. In 2004, the figure was 55 percent. Although in the southwest 59 percent of the population suffers under bitter poverty, in the North 76 percent does.[5]

The accelerating forces of the modern world—those of the West and of revolutionary Arabia—pull in different directions. In recent years, northern Nigeria has spawned ever more radical movements. Religious groups have risen up in rapid succession, only to disappear just as quickly. Charismatic preachers flare up brilliantly, but in short order fade away again. Boko Haram is the most recent and the most pernicious creature that the chaos in Nigeria has brought forth. The weaker the state, the stronger the extremist groups. And rarely has Nigeria been as weak as it is today.

What began as a small prayer group has evolved into a powerful army of an estimated 50,000 armed soldiers. More than 7 million displaced people are on the run. Many thousands have been enslaved. According to statements from the Nigerian government, to date twenty thousand people have died. Still, most deaths go uncounted in this conflict.

**Talatu:** I always pack my school bag the evening before. I take my English and math books, the book on agriculture, on integrated science, and an exercise book for lessons in Islam. I always take everything with me, regardless of what classes I have that day. That way I am always on the safe side. I only leave the books I need for Koran study at home, since we only have that on Fridays. I pack a few pens: a red, a blue, and a yellow one. I use the red one when the teacher gives a dictation. With the yellow one I solve problems. My school bag is small and white and made of cloth. I leave our house for the bus station with two friends from my class. Their names are Rukayya and Maimuna.

The school is in Gulak, a long way from my house, but sometimes we want to go by foot, not because we want to save money, but because it's fun. This way we have more time to talk with each other. By foot it takes us about an hour to get to school. But sometimes we just take a taxi. These are mopeds, always waiting at the side of the road. My school is called Central Bank Secondary School. Every Monday and Friday we have to stand in a row, and the teachers check to see if our fingernails are clean and trimmed. They check if our hair is combed and our clothes washed. The teachers are very strict. Despite this, I have always liked my teachers—except for one. He would hit you, and it didn't matter how small your mistake. He was our Koran teacher. Everyone was afraid of him. When he walked the hallway, we would run to our classrooms. The other teachers didn't like him either because he would criticize them for not being strict enough. He'd say, "Don't negotiate with the students: punish them! Don't engage with them." He hit us with a fan belt. His name was Aliyu Mallam.

I love to go on the swing at break, or to take the bike on a spin around the courtyard. For us, a bicycle is a special thing. We paid one student ten naira to ride for a bit on his. Such a feeling! I imagine riding a bike is a little like riding on a real horse.

To get home I usually take a moped taxi. I am usually tired. At home, my siblings have often eaten everything, so I cook once again, just for myself. Then I go with Mama to the bus stop and sell kosai.

The best moment of the day is just before I fall asleep. I feel so light.

When I am done with my schooling, I will marry. Not earlier. Only after. And then I want to be a doctor. I do not know anyone from my village who has become one. I don't know how I will become a doctor, what school I have to go to. But that is my dream.

**Sadiya:** The day Boko Haram came I awoke at three in the morning. It was a Friday. I cooked the rice, brought it to a woman who had a husking machine, and then dried it to sell at the market later on. Every morning after seeing the children off to school I would bake cakes. Every afternoon I'd go to the bus station to sell bean cakes until eleven at night. We made a good living this way, even without a man in the family. On this day, when I came home in the afternoon, I was tired, so I lay down on my raffia mat.

**Talatu:** This day I went as usual to school, came home, and took off my uniform. I made rice soup for myself and then I went over to Grandma's house to fetch some red beans for the soup. She said she saw injured soldiers running through the village. Boko Haram, she said, had already reached Gulak that morning. "You have to get to safety," Grandma said. "Boko Haram hunts down young girls like you."

In the short time Boko Haram has been in existence, it has gone through many metamorphoses. At first, the group was known under the name "Yusifiyya." This was a small group of orthodox believers and extremists who rallied around Mohammed Yusuf, a charismatic preacher. He was not an imam who had studied but a man of the people who could speak like no other. He fulminated against depravity and corruption. Yusuf lived in Maiduguri, a city of mud buildings and sheet-metal huts. It's estimated that before the conflict with Boko Haram 1.7 million people lived there. Today the population is said to be just shy of 3 million. In this city there are about five thousand mosques, a handful of these magnificent buildings with proud minarets. Most of Maiduguri's mosques, however, are as simple and humble as buildings in the rest of the city: one story, mud, and usually without windows.

Yusuf began to preach at his father-in-law's barn. It is said that in 2000 he broke with the Izala Movement, whose full name translates to Society for the Elimination of Heresy and Reestablishment of the Sunna.

Izala is Nigeria's first Islamic reform movement. Its preachers went from village to village in order to spread the word of Mohammed. Outside the urban centers people in the North lived according to centuries-old rituals. They were Muslim in name, but they actually prayed to gods of nature. They practiced fertility rituals and rain dances. The Izala movement fought against local traditions, which they wanted to replace uniformly with sharia, or Islamic law. At first, the Izala imams preached with great zeal and attracted to their ranks many young men who hoped for more freedom and self-determination, especially with respect to their parents. Young people rebelled against their elders. Yet as it became more successful, the movement merged with the ruling class of the North and became softer and more satisfied. Yusuf and his supporters were eager to implement much more radical ideas.

**Sadiya:** My little one, Buba, woke me where I was sleeping on my raffia mat. He was completely out of breath and said, "Boko Haram is coming! The soldiers are running away!" "You're lying," I said and stayed where I was. I mean, the military had just recently moved into our village with a lot of tanks. But then Talatu came in and told me the same thing. So I went to the door, and from there I could see the main street. I saw tanks racing down the street away from the village. Behind one of them ran a soldier with a boot in his hand. He was trying to leap onto the back of a tank. One of the tanks drove right into a roadside ditch, and the crew inside just left it there and ran away. I called my children to me and told them to take the sacks of beans to the storeroom, as well as the cooking pots from the kitchen— all the food. I locked all of our supplies in there. We took almost nothing with us, only the clothes on our backs.

I took Buba's hand and ran with him from our neighborhood. Behind us we heard cries of "Allahu Akbar." These cries drove us onward. The fighters stormed the village, and out of every house I saw people running. Everywhere, fleeing people. We just joined them, a great torrent of people. I saw people from Gulak and people from other villages in the area. I knew many of the faces. All of us ran.

**Talatu:** Mama said we must run. I had just enough time to fetch a clean dress and bring it with me. A fighter jet circled over the village, people running everywhere. We just followed them into the bush, away from the main street because that is where the Boko Haram men were. They did not follow us into the bush. That evening we reached a village in the mountains called Pallam. Our grandma, who had run away with us, had a cousin there. A Christian. We slept in his courtyard. But he said that we had to leave the next morning. Pallam is almost all Christian, and they now hate us Muslims because Boko Haram has killed so many Christians, and allegedly any Muslim is a supporter of Boko Haram. Early in the morning we went higher into the mountains, to the village of Zuyil, a Muslim village built into the cliffs. We slept there under a tree. Hundreds of people fled to the mountains.

**Sadiya:** For a while we were safe up there. But a boy from our village who knew the backcountry trails and the old escape routes of the people of Duhu led Boko Haram to us. This boy's name was Ibrahim. He is about fourteen years old. An orphan who grew up in the village without parents.

**Talatu:** I liked him. He was funny. His uncle's stand was at the same bus shelter as ours. Ibrahim and his uncle sold beef. And now this Ibrahim betrayed all of us. The Boko Haram fighters convinced him that anyone who fled was an infidel. They also gave him money. I heard that they later took him into the Sambisa, where he received training.

**Sadiya:** They came with bows and arrows to the mountain. They climbed the cliffs up to us. "You are Muslims!" they cried to us. "You do not need to be afraid!" What could we do? Our supplies up there on the mountain were running out.

The rise of Boko Haram began with a lie. In the early 2000s, the small radical group of the preacher Mohammed Yusuf attracted the attention of an important regional politician, Senator Ali Modu Sheriff. He was a member of the Nigerian parliament, son of a wealthy entrepreneur, and allied himself with Yusuf in order to win the gubernatorial elections in May 2003. The preacher Yusuf had attracted more and more followers. They adored him because he was incorruptible, because he said what he thought. Many of his followers had come to Maiduguri to be pupils at the Koranic schools; that is, parents handed over their children, some as young as six, as *almajiri*, to the care of a Muslim teacher, a *mallam*, because they had no money to feed them. There are ten thousand *almajiri* in Maiduguri. These children go to an Islamic school and then beg on the streets.

The ambitious senator who wanted to become governor made a pact with the radical preacher. Yusuf put his boys at the senator's disposal for the election. They campaigned for him, organized events, and intimidated opponents. In return, Sheriff assured Yusuf of financial support, a place in his provincial government, and full implementation of sharia law.

The sharia debate had convulsed the North at this point for fifteen years. This debate was not launched by radical preachers but by Muslim politicians. They said secular law was corrupt and had failed. Sharia law, however, would do away with corruption and tyranny. This is what the politicians promised, and the people believed them. All over north Nigeria governors organized moral vice squads that prohibited women from taking moped taxis (because they were driven by men not related to them) and scrutinized their clothing. Censorship authorities now watched over the local film industries. Politicians themselves, however, escaped the strictures of sharia. Corruption did not abate.

Sheriff campaigned for an even more radical program. He promised amputations and stonings for theft and adultery. Today, Sheriff insists vehemently that he never made an alliance with Yusuf or his followers. Yet Yusuf during this time became very wealthy and built his own mosque, which he named after Ibn Taymiyyah, a radical imam of the fourteenth century. Yusuf used his newfound wealth to offer his followers microcredit. They opened up small businesses. Sheriff is said to have given Yusuf fifty motorcycles, which his followers used to open transport businesses. Some of the revenue they generated returned to Yusuf's mosque and financed his organization. After his victory, Sheriff named a high-ranking member of Yusuf's group minister for religious affairs and thereby kept another promise. He showed much less enthusiasm, however, when it came to meeting his most important commitment: the full implementation of sharia law. State courts still employed national, secular law for serious crimes. Probably Sheriff had never intended to oppose the central government by proposing public stonings. His promise was probably no more than a trick.

After a few years the first fissures in the alliance between politician and preacher cracked open. Bitter, Yusuf pulled out of Sheriff's government. From that point on he railed against his former ally. He condemned him in public as an "apostate," as one who had turned away from the true faith. Yusuf and his followers became even more radical than they had been.

**Sadiya:** They forced us back to our villages. By the hundreds, they drove the women and children down into the valley. The next morning they gathered us together in the yard in front of the mosque. There, they forced all of us to convert to Islam, even those who already were Muslim. "Your Islam is not our Islam," a Boko Haram emir said to us. They call their leaders "emir." They held us prisoners in our own village for several days. We were allowed to go home but not out into the fields. At this point, most of the men had already fled into the bush. They left without the women, who might have slowed them down. Everybody knew that Boko Haram kills men without mercy.

**Talatu:** They came to the village in different kinds of cars. Many of them were new to me. One we called "Kirikou," after an evil spirit in a cartoon. It was a tank with a strange nose. They had a lot of Jeeps and pickup trucks. The fighters moved with their women into our houses. After a month they started marrying girls from the village. They said that they would marry every woman whose husband did not return within the month.

**Sadiya:** The men moved their headquarters to the marketplace, into the building where the Islamic school was. They hoisted their flag up. They had so many flags. Suddenly everywhere in the village there were flags. There were white flags with red letters, black flags with white letters. One read: "We have conquered the city of infidels!"

**Talatu:** "Pray!" they said to us. And we prayed in the square in front of the mosque. Hundreds of us. "You are not praying correctly!" they screamed at us. They said that when you bow forward it should not be just a little, but all the way, so that your entire upper body touches the ground. They said before their arrival we had not been proper Muslims. On the second day, they cut off the heads of two men in front of our eyes. One was a farmer, the other a farrier. Both had refused to become Muslim. The farrier screamed, "There is only one God! Our God is your God!"

They tied his hands with plastic straps, laid him on his belly, and began to cut his head off. He screamed, "Oh Jesus! Save me!" They cut the men's heads off with a big knife. They held the heads up by the ears and laid the dead out on their backs. So much blood—

**Sadiya:** They made new rules. Women were no longer allowed to fetch water, only children. I was no longer allowed to sell bean cakes. Women were no longer allowed to go to market alone. The Boko Haram men plundered our stores. Every day they took something from our houses. Every afternoon we were forced to attend Islamic studies in front of the mosque. After three weeks, an emir declared in that same place, "Tomorrow we will begin to marry you all to good Muslims." Talatu was standing next to me. They divided women into three categories: old women, middle aged, and young. I asked the emir, "Do you also want to marry off girls my daughter's age?" He answered by telling me that the prophet Mohammed took a seven-year-old girl as a wife. I said no more. With Boko Haram there is a moment when you know you have to be silent.

**Talatu:** I did not want to. I did not want to marry anyone yet. I cried and begged, "I will not marry! Please let us go home!"

**Sadiya:** We, the mothers from the village, decided to make another escape attempt the next night. To protect our girls. We made it to Pallam, the town in the foothills, but in the meantime the Christians had barricaded the village. They had an old hunting rifle and a lot of spears. They said they would kill us if we entered the village. In Pallam, Boko Haram had already killed many. In the other direction, Christians had also blocked our way. We'd heard that Christians waited there to waylay Muslims and drown them in a river. We had no choice. We returned to the village and Boko Haram.

**Talatu:** The fighters in the village did not know we had fled. Nobody saw us when we sneaked back into the village. But once again we were betrayed. They had a new spy. This time it was Ahmed. He was thirteen years old and lived like a stray dog. He did not go to school. He beat the little children in the village and stole their money. He picked on only the little children. His father sold red peppers at the market. Ahmed did not grow up with his parents but with his grandmother, who was pretty old. She was not able to control him. He was a friend of Ibrahim, the boy who had trapped us the first time.

The morning after we returned from our escape the fighters called us to the market square and announced that the boy Ahmed had helped them in their work for God. They said, "He informed us that you wanted to flee." The boy from that point onward was invulnerable. Ahmed was powerful, even though he didn't carry a gun. He strutted around the village, went anywhere he wanted, and no one dared to stop him. He reported everything to the militants. The boy said, "I am not afraid of soldiers anymore. I work for God now." He made sure we observed the new rules, that we wore the hijab, that we did not leave home without a veiled face. If the boy saw someone without a veil, he said nothing, just kept walking. But the next day during Koran lessons at the market square you'd be beaten out in the open.

This is how they doled out the beatings. If you broke a rule for the first time, you'd be warned but not beaten. If you broke the rule a second time, they still didn't whip you. The third time, they whipped you three times. For the fourth violation, they did not beat you, and also not for the fifth. If caught in a violation for the sixth time, they whipped you six times. And that's how they kept counting. The morning after Ahmed had betrayed us, they whipped every girl my age ten times. Women the age of my mother they beat fifteen times. Children younger than I they whipped five times. Children under four they did not beat at all. That is law under Boko Haram.

When it was my turn, they blindfolded me. They held my arm. I had to open my hand. They gave me five lashes with a stick on one hand, and five on the other. When they realize you are about to cry, they don't strike so hard.

Boko Haram wants to create a caliphate with a sword. For the most part their caliphate is a vague concept that is best put into focus by considering the villages they have held for some time. Almost inevitably, their rule begins with murder. The fighters kill those who might pose a danger to them—young men who worked for security forces or refused to join Boko Haram. They kill clerics who contradict their interpretation of Islam. Soon after that, they choose an emir to govern the village and surrounding areas. How much this emir intervenes in the everyday lives of the village varies from place to place. In some villages it seems the emir just wants to look after his soldiers, leaving civilian life for the most part untouched. In other places, the emirs establish courts that settle disputes, implement sharia law, and distribute food and medicine. In most cases, the emir comes from the village he governs. The emirs have also changed place-names. For example, Gwoza, the group's capital, is now Darul Hikma (Home of Wisdom). The new bosses take the houses of the old bosses, commandeer the villas of the rich, and turn them into their headquarters. They live from that which they plunder in their newly conquered realm.

On the first day after taking a village or area, Boko Haram leaders gather all the people together who have not fled or been killed. In a central square, the emir lays down the new laws, according to which, for example, the purchase and consumption of cigarettes are declared against Islam and forbidden. Drugs of any kind are prohibited. Men are commanded to grow their hair and beards. A new dress code is announced: white trousers, which are not to touch the ground, for men, and full-body covering for the women. The village markets are reorganized. Boko Haram forbids middlemen. The producer is allowed to sell only directly to the consumer, the consumer to buy only directly from the producer. The movement of women beyond the village is restricted. Even men need to acquire passes from the emir to make trips between villages. Since women don't work—indeed, they are all but shackled to house and home—and since most men (those who have not fled or been killed) are forced to fight with Boko Haram, it is the children who do most of the work in the realm of Boko Haram. They work the fields and gather firewood.

Slaves are the foundation upon which Boko Haram is attempting to erect its empire. The Islamic sect forces young men into fighting its battles and marries off young girls. They enslave older women as laborers. The logistics of mass rape depend on a network of camps that Boko Haram maintains. The camps, often located in the hometowns of the prisoners, can have hundreds of women. They serve as places where women can be observed, made submissive, and forced to study Islam. As needed, women are moved from one camp to the other. For the girls who are chosen to carry out suicide attacks, there are special "training centers." If Boko Haram suffers a defeat, the women are carted off as part of the military retinue. Women are the currency with which Boko Haram leaders buy the loyalty of their subordinates. The emirs decide who is allowed to reproduce with whom. Women are merely receptacles for Boko Haram genes. The men want their children to be raised completely in the spirit of their movement.

It is not known when the group that had coalesced around Yusuf started to call itself Boko Haram for the first time. In the first years of its existence, the movement had no name. Yusuf was jailed a few times for his inflammatory sermons, which explicitly condemned the secular state and the people who ruled it. He was nonetheless always released after a short period. It was assumed that Sheriff and other politicians still protected him. Their reasons are unclear. Did Yusuf know too much? Did he threaten to oppose them even more aggressively?

Eventually, Yusuf's movement branched out. In 2003, shortly

after the elections, sixty to seventy of his followers, men in their twenties, left Maiduguri, which they deemed impure at that point. They moved westward, into open territory, to the neighboring state of Yobe, a sparsely populated place where they would shun society. They found their way to an island in a boundary river between Niger and Nigeria and fashioned there a new world, far from all distractions, a place where they could be closer to God. This group was not dominated by the *almajiris* anymore but by the sons of rich families, among them the nephew of the governor of Yobe, who had allocated this land for them. They called their encampment "Afghanistan" and raised the flag of the Taliban.

Yusuf had inspired this camp, but others led it. For the first time, we hear the name Abubakar Shekau, the man who would become Yusuf's successor. An even more important figure during this time was one Mohammed Ali, who had studied Islam in the Sudanese capital Khartoum and there became a follower of Osama bin Laden. According to the International Crisis Group, he is reckoned to have accompanied bin Laden to Afghanistan, from where he is said to have returned to Maiduguri in 2002 with three million dollars.[6] In two audio messages from 2000 and 2002, bin Laden addressed the Muslims of Nigeria and tried to incite rebellion.[7]

His meeting with Ali, the Afghanistan veteran, strongly influenced Yusuf. Until that time, Yusuf had preached nonviolent resistance, but this changed after he had met Ali. The time of peaceful retreat on the river island was over. The men on the island had arguments with inhabitants of the surrounding villages over fishing rights. When the villagers brought in the police, religious zeal caught fire. In December 2003, the group attacked the security forces, stole their weapons, and took over guard stations in the surrounding area. The rampage lasted ten days.

Did their isolation on the island reaffirm their belief that they were close to God and ultimate truth? Did they now fancy themselves invincible? The details are not clear. What we do know is that this uprising ended in catastrophe for Yusuf's group. For two days Nigerian troops lay siege to "Camp Afghanistan," and most of Yusuf's followers were killed. Mohammed Ali, bin Laden's alleged ambassador, escaped and at first sought refuge at a friendly imam's house. The police found him there and killed him. Yusuf fled to Saudi Arabia, supposedly to devote himself to religious studies, but returned two years later under the auspices of Yobe's governor. The survivors of "Camp Afghanistan" now formed the militant core of the "Yusuf" movement. They vowed vengeance against the state.

**Sadiya:** They drove ten trucks into the village and parked them one behind the other at the market square. The emir ordered us to get in. All the young women of Duhu. Only the elderly were allowed to stay. The emir was named Man Bakura, a Kanuri from Maiduguri. A tall, fat man. He never hit us, but instead ordered others to hit us. He was the one who gave the order to kill the two Christians. We begged the fighters to let us stay, we promised we would never again try to run away, we would always stay here and wait for them. Most of the women cried. All around us stood men with whips. They hit the women who struggled and shot their guns into the air. When they shot, we climbed onto the trucks. One after the other, they drove off. Talatu and I got on the flatbed. They didn't tell us where it was going, but we knew. Into the forest.

We drove to a city called Gwoza, near the forest. They said we were staying the night and locked us in a house and finally gave us something to eat. Our legs hurt. We were so thirsty. The men brought us mats to sleep on, mats they had stolen from the abandoned houses. There were not enough for everyone, and we had no blankets. A woman complained. She was from Gulak and the only one who defied the fighters. She did not keep quiet. She complained a lot. Now she complained about the blankets. A fighter shot her in the shin. She fell to the ground bleeding and screamed. The hut's clay floor was full of blood. A few women helped her up and bandaged her. The next morning she was taken to a doctor. At least that's what the men said. I never saw her again. I don't know whether she really was taken to a doctor or not. Then we were loaded onto the trucks again.

Five gates lead into the Sambisa. Ropes are stretched across the entrances, and a metal plate with Arabic figures hangs from them. These are the markers of Boko Haram. Officially, the Sambisa is a national park. In the 1990s, it still attracted tourists and large-game hunters who paid to be there. The state park administration had nineteen chalets built, a restaurant, and an information center with satellite antennae. A total of fifty rangers were supposed to be able to protect the forest. They were supposed to scare poachers and hunt down people who steal firewood. Small groups of seven men each were distributed in a network of stations throughout the forest and coordinated from a headquarters led by a chief ranger. On February 5, 2013, a Boko Haram commando attacked the ranger headquarters, killed two rangers, and forced the others to flee. Also, the villages bordering the Sambisa have since then been abandoned. To come too close to the forest is to risk your life.

**Sadiya:** The branches of the trees whipped us as we drove through the forest. When the truck drove past a nest of wild wasps, it fell down on us and they stung us. Eventually, the vehicle stopped at a place where the route narrowed to a trail. We had to get out for an hour; we walked in a long column.

**Talatu:** We came to a stand of old trees where women and children were camped out. They call this place "Gate 1." The leaves on the trees are very thick here. When it rains, you don't notice it at all. One of the fighters—I think it was the emir—spoke to us: "You are now like the Chibok girls. You will stay here forever." Then they showed us where we would sleep. The fighters then assigned us a tree. At the camp a tree is like a house. Many young shoots grow around the trunk so that it is always cold and moist. We lay down and it was like being in a cave. I think that's why we have this bad cough.

**Sadiya:** I was afraid of the tree. There were so many snakes in it. We broke branches off the tree and covered the ground with them and then lay our clothes on top. It was a shea tree. They have long shiny leaves that look like green tongues.

A second family lived with us, Amina and her two children. The whole trip long, Amina had already had diarrhea. On the second evening, she went a few meters into the forest to relieve herself. She took a long time, so I roused myself and looked for her. I found her on the ground. A snake had bitten her. The Sambisa has flying snakes. They jump from branch to branch. I asked two of the Boko Haram fighters to help me drag her back to the tree. I cared for her the whole night. She squirmed and screamed. She begged for water. I gave her water. She started to bleed from her ears and her nose. Her mouth filled with white froth. The next morning she was dead. "Look after my children," she said before dying. I promised her I would. Amina had a boy who was four and a girl who was five. The fighters took her body with them. They also took the children. What they did with them, I do not know. The fighters told me they took the children to the Chibok girls. I often ask Amina in my dreams for forgiveness because I was not able to keep my promise.

The hour of the death of Boko Haram's founder was also the hour of Boko Haram's birth. In the early evening hours of July 30, 2009, Mohammed Yusuf was at a large military base in Maiduguri, naked above the waist and handcuffed. Excited men in uniform crowded around him, filming him with their cell phones, filming the last minutes of his life.

A month before, a procession of Yusuf's followers came to a roadblock manned by a special task force. Yusuf's followers were outside of Maiduguri on the way to a funeral. The task force had allegedly stopped them because they were not wearing motorcycle helmets. A few months before, the government had made wearing helmets while on a motorcycle a legal requirement, though this law was rarely enforced. But on this day it was. Yusuf's men refused to cooperate. There was a tussle. Insults were exchanged, and eventually there were gunshots. The details are disputed. In the end, three of the preacher's men were dead, and seventeen more were injured. Yusuf wrote an open letter to the government demanding a dialogue within the next forty days. The deadline passed, and the next step was open war. On July 26 at 10 p.m., Yusuf's followers attacked multiple sites around Maiduguri. They had bows and arrows, knives, hoes, and firearms. They attacked police stations and the homes of police officers, then tried to break into the security forces' armories. They set churches on fire and stormed the central prison, freeing the inmates and killing the guards. That night they killed 32 police, cutting their throats. By early morning, Yusuf's men controlled a large portion of the city. But then the military sent reinforcements. On the twenty-eighth and twenty-ninth of July, the army shot at Yusuf's mosque complex and killed dozens of his followers. Two days later, he was tracked down in his father-in-law's chicken stall.

In the end, Yusuf lay in his own blood, his hands still cuffed. A bullet had split open his skull. Brain mass was exposed. In the photographs taken at the time, you can see bullet holes to the stomach, chest, and his upper and lower arms. His death was an execution. An independent investigation never took place. Government forces probably thought that with his death the whole movement would finally be destroyed. However, the opposite was true, for the militants were soon stronger than ever. The group went underground. From that time we have practically no information about its leadership. Less is known about Boko Haram than the leaders of North Korea. In the months following Yusuf's death, Boko Haram turned into a beast, and one of the most bizarre terrorist leaders in the world became its head: Abubakar Shekau. After the fighting in Maiduguri ended, the Nigerian military also announced Shekau's death. Then, in mid-2010, he was back with his own message: "Here is Shekau, Shekau, Shekau, Shekau, the one and only," he exulted. "I want the world to know that I am alive, by the grace of God."

**Sadiya:** The children gradually became sick. Estha was already sick by the time we'd reached the camp. She had stomach problems. Buba's chest hurt. The men always sent him to fetch water, to a creek that was far from the camp. They sent most of the children to collect water. The children needed over an hour to get there and then another hour to return.

**Talatu:** In the camp, we always woke up at about four in the morning. If they had plundered the nearby villages sufficiently, we'd have something to eat. Many days we had nothing. From time to time the fighters would bring back an animal that they'd shot in the forest—a deer, a gazelle, or a wild boar. One time they even brought back a zebra. There were a lot of monkeys: baboons that ran around on the ground and others that we heard only, high above us in the leaves.

I often could not sleep. At night I heard the young boys sing-song mumbling. They were there to guard us. The whole night through they read the Koran aloud. These boys were between eight and ten years old. They had to read it out loud. The fighters forced them to do this. They wanted the boys to learn the Koran quickly so that they could be sent into battle. They read the Koran from beginning to end. Once they'd read the whole thing, the men gave them a gun.

At night in the camp there were so many strange voices. Crying, shouting, and loud screeches. The "hee-hee-hee" sound was terrible. A sound like the whinnying of a horse.

Boko Haram has divided the forest encampment into two halves. In the front half, the kidnapped women and their children slept. The youngest Boko Haram fighters, many no older than thirteen, watched over them. In the rear of the camp were married women who had willingly joined Boko Haram and its fighters. There, right at the edge of the camp, was the only permanent building. This was Abubakar Shekau's house. The roof and walls were made of glistening corrugated iron. They gleamed silver in the twilight of the forest.

Shekau, the new leader of Boko Haram, was even more radical than his mentor, Mohammed Yusuf. Shekau began Boko Haram's reign of terror. He is a bearded man who, in his video messages, often wears a pointed wool cap. His videos are different from those of al-Qaida or ISIS. He often loses his composure. There is nothing dignified about him. He squints his eyes together in hatred, leans in to the camera, as though he wants to crawl right up into the person watching. He threatens, shouts, drools, breaks into raucous laughter, grins with malice. He doesn't just announce the cruelties Allah has apparently asked him to carry out. He relishes them with every gesture. Strangely, these videos are frightening, even when one watches them in an office in Europe. Shekau does not want to appear as an imam. Rather, he takes on the guise of a sorcerer.

Details of Shekau's life are hard to come by. Some sources say he is in his late thirties, some say he is in his mid-forties. By some accounts, he is from the village of Shekau on the border with Niger. Others dispute this and insist he was born in Niger. The government of Niger, in turn, denies this. What we do know is that like Yusuf he came to Maiduguri as an *almajiri*, begging on the streets and loitering around mosques. He rose through the ranks of Islamic students and ultimately married the daughter of a preacher, with whom he also lived. According to reports, his wife died giving birth to their first child. This apparently changed him markedly. He became so violent that at times he needed to be restrained with chains. After Yusuf's death, Shekau married one of his mentor's four widows and adopted her children.

None of the women with whom we spoke had ever seen him. He lived in his silver hut only when he visited the camp. His actual hideaway was deeper in the forest. The Nigerian military announced his death on a few more occasions in 2009. However, it is unclear whether he is still alive or whether others who bear a resemblance to him now perform his role. Myths have sprouted up around Shekau's name, myths that have their roots not in Islam but in a time that comes long before it. People say he has magical powers, the ability to make himself invisible. He has bound hostages to the forest with his magic.

**Sadiya:** Shekau's wife always slept in his house. She was about forty, not as young as the wives of the other fighters. There were guards assigned just to her and the house. Two of the kidnapped Chibok girls were given to her as servants. The Chibok girls cooked for her, washed her things. We saw his wife in the kitchen only when Shekau was visiting. Two plastic chairs stood in front of the hut, the only two chairs in the camp. They looked like thrones, for a king and queen. One was yellow and bigger than the other. This was for Shekau. The other was green and meant for his wife.

**Talatu:** The Chibok girls lived even deeper in the forest than we did with Shekau. That's what the girls told us. I do not know where. We saw them as they came out of the underbrush along a narrow path. Around two in the afternoon they would come, always two of them, the Boko Haram fighters guarding them. These girls gave us lessons in Islam. The camp's mosque was just open ground. Pebbles had been poured on the ground to make a rectangle, which was meant to be the prayer room. The Chibok girls were very strict. They whipped us on the back with plastic cables if we were not able to read the Koran in Arabic. "We were also kidnapped," they told us. "But you have to get over it. You are carrying out the work of God here."

For the most part the Chibok girls had no time to talk with us. They came, taught us Islam for two hours, and left. When the military advanced on the forest, they did not visit anymore. From that point on, a kid of about sixteen was our teacher. He would hit us over nothing. Not only me, my mother, too.

Once, four girls wanted to flee. They ran away when they heard the military was near to the forest. But they made a mistake: they did not flee through the underbrush, but on a path. That's where they ran straight into the arms of the Boko Haram; they were taken to Shekau to be killed. That's what the fighters told us. We never saw them again.

**Sadiya:** On our second day at the camp, I was married to a fighter. One of Shekau's deputies came to me with a stranger. He pointed to me and said, "That's your wife." Both men smiled, and I was terribly afraid. I stayed quiet. They held a ceremony in the camp mosque, but I wasn't present. I heard about it from the fighter who brought me the dowry. This amounted to two thousand naira (*about nine euros*). The man I had to marry was named Ali. He was about my age. He spoke Kanuri. Later, he told me that before the war he was a student of the Koran, one of those who beg on the street. Sometimes we spoke normally to one another, but then later I again would feel only hate for this man.

He moved to be with us under the tree. I did everything he wanted. If I didn't sleep with him, he'd tell the emir. I often pretended to be sick so that I would not have to be with him. In the first few weeks I did not speak with him. I refused to smile at him. So he had his friends flog me. I received fifteen strokes from a cable. After that, I tried to be friendlier to him.

I know a woman who refused to have sex with the man she was forced to marry. She said she wanted a proper wedding, not that pitiful ritual in the forest. I watched as they brought this woman to Shekau's hut, and as, a little later, they dragged away her corpse. I'd had a lot of conversations with her. She told me how she had two children, and how she did not want to bear any more because she'd almost died during her last delivery. Her name was Aischa, and she was from the village of Gubla. Her husband was a bricklayer.

**Talatu:** I was married off to the assistant teacher. The emir Abu Zahra came to me and told me I am old enough to marry. If you refuse, he said, we will take you to the Chibok girls, and they will kill you. I do not know anymore when I was married to that man. The assistant teacher always beat us especially hard during our lessons. The men held the ceremony in the mosque, without me. I was then separated from my mother and taken to a camp called "Gate 2," which was deeper in the forest. Here, the trees stood together more densely than at the first camp. I missed my mother terribly.

I do not remember how the man who was my husband looked. I do not know anymore. I have already forgotten almost everything.

(*a long silence*)

I was lucky. He wasn't able to harm me.

Talatu does not want to remember anything, and we do not ask any more questions. Perhaps she does remember but would rather remain silent. Women who have been raped in the region are usually ostracized. They are deemed dishonored and sullied. If it is known that they have been raped, they will often not find a husband, which is often the only way of securing a financial future. Such women live on the margins of society.

Sadiya and Talatu eventually escaped the camp in June 2015 during a military raid. Time and again the military attack the forest, but the generals are reluctant to take risks, rarely sending in foot soldiers. Instead, they fight from a safe distance, with fighter aircraft, helicopters, and heavy artillery. The camps were recklessly and ruthlessly bombarded, even though they knew that mostly women and children lived there. Time and again the military celebrated its campaign with reports of success, announcing that they had freed women from the forest. Indeed, with their attacks, they did help many hostages to escape, but they possibly also killed more women and children than they liberated.

**Sadiya:** The day we escaped was almost worse than the day of our abduction. It was as though the world was burning down. Fire in the trees. Bombs. Behind us and in front of us. We ran. We ran. We fled together with all the women from Duhu. A hundred women and children from Duhu. We knew more or less what direction to run—to the southeast! We took our bearings by the sun, but we were often not able to see it because the canopy was so thick above us. After a few hours we came across a group of grass huts clustered together in the underbrush. They were skeletal frameworks made from bare branches on top of which wilted leaves had been laid. As we came nearer, strange women emerged from them. "Where are you going this late at night?" they asked. "We are running away!" we cried. "We've been kidnapped!" They allowed us to stay the night with them.

**Talatu:** I don't know who these women were. As far as I remember, there were about fifteen. They had tribal markings on their cheeks. Half the huts were empty. They were built the way the Fulani make them.

Fulani nomads were the first victims of the resurgent Boko Haram. When the jihadists were defeated during their 2009 uprising, they were at first too weak to confront security forces on the streets. Instead, they took to the paths of the nomads. These ancient routes along which the Fulani drove their cattle are not watched over by anyone and usually pass villages at a distance: a street network in the shadows. Boko Haram fighters could drive along these routes from place to place without resistance, and this is how Fulani culture fell doubly victim to them.

The Islamic sect was able to find many supporters among the Fulani, especially young men, who, with the help of the insurgents, rebelled against older generations. They no longer accepted the subordinate role they had to their elders and tried to destroy the culture of their parents. Before the war, the Fulani followed the rain with their herds and wandered almost as far as Niger. Today, their cattle paths are barely passable. The danger of being assaulted by one of the many clashing groups in this conflict is too great.

As though out of nowhere Boko Haram would attack villages. Lying in ambush, they shot police officers whom they believed to have participated in the deaths of their fellow terrorists. The fighters killed prison guards they accused of torture, gunned down village leaders who had turned over Boko Haram followers to security forces. The assassins usually shot victims as they drove past. More and more, Boko Haram expanded its circle of victims. In December 2010 they carried out for the first time a bomb attack in Abuja, the Nigerian capital.

**Talatu:** The women spoke a language we did not speak. They knew only broken Hausa. What they spoke sounded like Fulani. They said, "Our men brought us here. You can sleep here, but then you've got to keep going. We don't want any trouble." They had sheep and a donkey.

**Sadiya:** Just before sunrise we were on the move again. The women were creepy. I think they were married to Boko Haram men. But we didn't know. Anyway they didn't harm us. The second night we spent under a tree. We sat the whole night against its trunk and did not dare lie down because of the insects. All around us on the ground were these huge, brown ants. And they bit! The third night we came across traces of people: a group of empty houses. We saw a lot of footprints, and in the houses we saw calabashes and plastic jugs. They looked as though someone might use them from time to time. While it was still dark we left this place because we were afraid that it might be a Boko Haram hideout. The fourth night we slept in high grass. Around us were only solitary, low trees. We had left the forest behind us and reached the swamps. The entire next day we trudged through them, but by evening we were again on solid ground. The ground was dry red sand, just like in my village. On the fifth day we saw a cell tower, the first sign that we were near the main road. All one hundred women who had fled with us reached Duhu. No one can say God does not love us. His hand protected all of us.

**Talatu:** We now live with our grandma in Duhu. But this is no good. There is no one who protects us. Many people give us evil looks. My half brother is still in the forest. He is thirteen. The villagers say he is fighting now for Boko Haram. But they carried him off just as they did us and forced him to join them. When I was still in the forest I asked the Chibok girls about him. They said he had been taken to a training camp. My half brother is named Abubakar. He is a good boy, a funny boy. I don't want anyone to hurt him.

**Sadiya:** I am pregnant by my Boko Haram husband and want to have the child. I do not want to kill it. I do not want to be guilty in the eyes of God. Many people tell me to get an abortion. Men who make up the village's Christian defense militia come to our house and say that if it is a boy they will kill him because he will only join Boko Haram. That's what they say, anyway. They say I lived with Boko Haram. They say my thirteen-year-old son fights with Boko Haram. Now my village says I am one of them. I went to the military and complained about what the militia had said. The army outposts in my village support me. There are, after all, many women in the village like me. But the head of the militia came to me once again. He warned me that the military would soon be leaving, but they, the militia, would stay. Everyone asks me now what I am going to do.

There is a long silence as she looks at the floor.

**Sadiya:** I don't know.

"My brothers, you should take slaves. I kidnapped girls from a school, and you are irritated. I say, we must stop the spread of Western education. I kidnapped the girls. I will sell them on the market, with Allah's help. There is a market where one can sell humans. Allah has told me to sell them. He commands me to sell them. I will sell women. I sell women."

—*Abubakar Shekau, April 2014*

# THE TREE

Batula is Sadiya's older sister. The forty-one-year-old woman has nine children. Strong and with an open face, she tries to make eye contact, unlike her sister. She wants me to understand her and speaks quickly. Batula has come with her thirteen-year-old daughter, Rabi. She suckles a two-week-old boy. She was pregnant when Boko Haram abducted her. We meet in a kind of garden house on the crest of a hill in Yola. Security guards protect the land around the small wooden house. The house's walls are ventilated on all sides so that its interior is pleasantly cool. A gentle wind wafts through. From outside, low music from a radio drifts in. We hear the cackling of chickens. Two geckos, one big and one small, one with red feet, the other with yellow, scurry fitfully over the walls. Now and then one of them appears near me, very near, very suddenly, and I am startled. That is when the women laugh. I love these geckos because they make them laugh.

Batula's husband worked on a plantation managing several field laborers until Boko Haram attacked. She sold red beans, rice, and corn at the market. She lived in Gubla, a village of ten thousand on the A13 highway. Her husband is still missing, as is her eldest daughter. In her family, seventeen people have been killed by Boko Haram or the military. Rabi is very delicate. During the course of our conversation, she either sleeps or sits on a raffia mat and stares in front of her.

Batula lived for nine months in camp "Gate 1," a few trees distant from her sister Sadiya. Rabi was separated from her mother and imprisoned in camp "Gate 2," where she saw Talatu in the Islamic school but was forbidden from talking to her.

**Batula:** I do not want to bore you. Tell me if I am boring you because there's nothing special about my story. I was born in Gubla. My parents were farmers and planted sugarcane on the river. When my father was a boy, he held the old beliefs still. He came from Sukur, in the mountains. He had a tough childhood. His mother died when he was nine. When my grandfather married again, the new woman chased away my father. He begged in the village. Then, a family of Fulani nomads took him in. For many years he wandered with them. They were Muslim, so he became Muslim. As a young man he had had enough of the sorcery and the rituals in which one must dance naked. He was the only one in his family to convert to Islam. Everyone else in our family became Christian.

People had just begun to settle in the valley. That's why my father had to first cultivate a piece of land. He was among the first to build in this part of Gubla. Now his land has become a part of the city, with many houses and stores. Before the Boko Haram crisis began, the price of land had gone up quite a lot.

My mother and he had five children together, and then they divorced. We stayed in father's house because among our people children always belong to the father. Then he married a new woman. In our tribe, stepchildren have a tough life. The new wives don't like them. So we children cooked separately from the rest of the family. Our father only secretly let us have salt because otherwise his new wife would have fought with him, and he did not want any tension. No more divorce for him. The stepmother had total control of the house. Our mother went back to her family in Duhu and took only my sister Sadiya with her because she was the youngest. My father divorced my mother because she bore him only girls. His friends said, "Get divorced. When you die and you leave behind only girls then everything you have made of your life will fall apart." So he left her. And the new wife gave him nine daughters! You can't force the hand of God!

———

She laughs, shakes her head, laughs again, and then dries her tears.

**Batula:** When I was the age of my oldest daughter, who is seventeen, I married my half brother's friend. I liked him. He worked hard and made sure we had food. I also liked the way he moved, the way he walked. Every move seemed to involve dancing.

He was a merchant. He'd buy beans from farmers in Gubla and sell them in Maiduguri. He sold five different kinds of beans. That went well for a few years, but then everything went wrong. Four years ago, one of his clients from the South bought 150 dollars' worth of beans on credit and disappeared. My husband looked all over for him but never found him. A bit later he was robbed on the road from Madagali to Gubla. He was in a share taxi when thieves posing as passengers got in. They stole 800,000 naira (*3,600 euros*) from him and disappeared. He gave up after that. He didn't have the nerve for it anymore. He borrowed 250,000 naira from friends and bought tools and seeds. He became a farmer, hiring up to fifteen workers from the mountains around Sukur. They come cheap. You pay them ten thousand naira (*about 50 euros*) a year and supply them with free food. For that they work without stopping. My husband worked in the fields far away from the village. He worked hard and soon he was able to pay off his debts. He lived in the bush, and I lived in the village. I saw him only a few days a month.

I think he loved me. In all those years, he never brought another woman home. I sold what he grew in the field at the market: beans, rice, corn. We had enough money. We had a good life.

Gubla is one of the last of the large villages before the Sambisa. So it was also one of the first villages Boko Haram attacked. The fighters could strike quickly and then hurry back into the forest. Gubla, the home of two thousand people, is divided in itself. Members of different tribes moved from the hinterlands to live here, Christians as well as Muslims. Boko Haram found supporters here early on. Those who attacked the village from without actually came from within.

This region has two worlds: the mountain and the valley. Like almost all the villages in the valley, Gubla was founded in the 1920s during British colonial rule. Before that, most people lived in the mountains. For centuries, they had entrenched themselves there because down in the valleys life was too dangerous. Every few years, slave hunters from the large kingdoms of Kanuri and Fulani would sweep out of the North. Until late in the nineteenth century, the slave trade was one of the most important sources of income. Only a small fraction of slaves were shipped off to America. The majority remained in West Africa and served the urban elite of the old kingdoms. Their wealth was based on slavery.

The slave raids profoundly shaped the region's culture since this time. Men and women have scarified faces so that in case of abduction they can recognize each other's tribes. The Germans, who governed parts of this territory from their colony in Cameroon, tried in vain to stop the slave raids. Only the British, who took over the territory after the First World War, succeeded in putting a stop to it in the 1920s. Still, only generations later did people in the mountains feel safe enough to settle in the fertile valleys.

**Rabi:** I am in the fifth grade here in Gubla. I am the second best in my class. I don't like school so much. Our school is not especially good. I like our English teacher because he always arrives on time. Most come late or not at all. My school is right next to our house. This is good because that way I am never late. There are thirty-six children in my class. Our classroom has four windows, but they have no panes. But that doesn't matter. When it rains, we push our benches farther into the room. We jump rope during break. We play with empty milk cans that we nailed to cardboard wheels. We pretend the cans are cars. We race them around the school yard. My friends are called Bilkis, Baby, and Biya. We eat together and play together and fetch water together. We four do almost everything together. I miss them very much.

**Batula:** I am happy that Rabi goes to school. I don't want my children to have my life. My father did us no favors by forbidding us from going to school. If I had gone to school, my life would be better now. I would be a teacher or a nurse. I am not dumber than they are, but I can't write and can only read a little. I have nine children: four sons and five daughters. One daughter is still in the forest. She is sixteen. One of my sons died in an accident. He was nine. We were brewing beer at home and a pot exploded. It was winter. We were cooking up the millet in a big pot to ferment it later. Many children sat around the fire because it was so cold that day. My son was right in front of it. The hot millet poured over him and he died.

In Gubla we have eight churches, five mosques, and two Koranic schools. We have a large market. Our village was once very safe. Of course, we also had a few thieves, but they came from other villages. They lived in the mountains and came to steal from us in the valley. In Gubla itself we only had a few children who would steal grain from the stores.

I can well remember the last peaceful day in the village. It was a Friday at the end of August. We had had a good week at the market. Market days are from Tuesday to Thursday. My daughter, the one still with Boko Haram in the forest, helped me to push our carts of vegetables to the market. Before I begin selling my goods, I pray to God for success. God was very good to us that week. The price of beans was at 350 naira (*about 1.60 euros*) for two kilograms. That is a very good price. Sometimes you can sell them for just 150 naira. But at the time food was scarce because of the fighting going on. I made 32,000 naira at the market that week.

In the evening we celebrated with juicy beef. I was nervous because every few days I heard gunshots—sometimes here, sometimes there, but mostly at the edge of town. Yet the people said, "Boko Haram will not take our village. What would they want here? We have nothing." On Wednesday of that week a few people had fled the village, above all the rich. But the village was still quiet. On Thursday it was peaceful, and on Friday, too. The pastor had said in his sermon the previous week that he would flee to the south with his children. His congregation is Protestant and called "Deeper Life Church." Most of its members followed the pastor. The leader of the Koranic school also fled with him. They were good friends. You could see them walking together in Gubla.

**Rabi:** Our teachers said on the day before the attack that they would flee Gulak, but they didn't say when. They had us copy texts to do with mathematics and agriculture. That was all we did on that last day. When we were done, we went home.

**Batula:** On the day Boko Haram came we were, as always, out in the fields. We had to plant beans. We couldn't wait any longer. It was early morning, about six. As we were walking along a path to the field, we heard gunshots. They came from the village. I told the children to hide in the bush and that I would go back to the village to fetch the rest of the family. I was so afraid, but I could not leave my children behind! On the way to the village I already saw the fighters. They wore camouflage uniforms and turbans on their heads. They shot at all the men, even if they were unarmed. I saw that. I saw how they shot at men who tried to flee on mopeds. The mopeds tipped over, and the men were dead. On the way to town, I saw eleven dead bodies. Then I reached our house and took the children with me into the bush.

A fighter jet raced over us and fired its guns into the village. Just like that, without aiming. In my eldest daughter's house nine people died: the first wife's three children, the husband's mother, and five other relatives who had just fled another village to find safety in Gubla. Two women and three children. Once I had made it to the mountains with my children, a Gubla woman told me that the jet had killed my daughter. I left all my children with this woman and hurried back down to the village. I waited for a moment for the shooting to stop. The fighters had sped away on their motorcycles to a different village. On the way to her house I saw her, my daughter—alive! She was tired, but she was alive! We cried and hugged each other. We stood in front of her destroyed house. I saw a leg, ripped from its body, on top of the ruins. The streets were filled with so many dead. Most had died at the hands of Boko Haram. With my own eyes I saw forty-three corpses.

For a long time, Nigeria's centers of power did not take Boko Haram seriously. This country is acquainted with many horrors. Thousands die every year in its big cities. They are killed in robberies, in the conflicts between street gangs in Lagos. The front pages report stories about occult ritual murders in which sometimes dozens die. In the Christian South, radical Protestants demand that children possessed by the devil be killed. Boko Haram, and its terrorist murders, which began in 2010 and 2011, was just one horror among many. Jihadist militants in the distant northeast of the country were not part of the national debates. That changed when the new Boko Haram leader Abubakar Shekau decided to take the fight to the capital. He had his followers do what to that point in Nigeria had been unimaginable. On June 16, 2011, a well-to-do businessman, Mohammed Manga, blew himself up in a Honda in front of police headquarters in Abuja. This was the first suicide attack in the history of the country. The thirty-five-year-old Manga was from Maiduguri, attended Mohammed Yusuf's sermons, and flew often on business to the United Arab Emirates. He is supposed to have left his five children four million naira (about 18,000 euro). He killed five police officers but missed his main target: the general inspector of the Nigerian police.

Only two months later, Boko Haram's name splashed across international headlines. On August 26, 2011, a twenty-seven-year-old mechanic, Mohammed Abdul Barra, drove into the UN headquarters with a truck full of explosives. The explosion killed twenty-five UN employees and more than a hundred people were injured. "I know it will be very painful for you to lose me, my mother," Barra said in a video he recorded before his death. "It was my love of God that told me to obey you, and it is this same Allah who commands me to carry out this mission."

These spectacular acts of terror were meant to have internal effects as well as external ones. They were part of a recruiting strategy. Conservative Muslims were meant to have the impression that Boko Haram was capable, that it was a powerful messenger from God. Soon, Boko Haram had consolidated itself to such an extent that it had the power to terrorize the entire Muslim North of Nigeria.

For example, on a single day of coordinated attacks in Kano, the capital of the state of the same name, 185 people were killed. Between June 2011 and January 2012, Boko Haram followers burned down eighteen churches in eight northern states. They killed 127 Christians. In a video message in January 2012, Shekau said he was "at war" with Christians.

The sect's actions sent more and more shock waves across the country. Security forces took on Boko Haram with renewed vigor. They jailed many of its members, as well as a few leaders, who have by now disappeared. The Nigerian military often acted with more cruelty than Boko Haram. Human rights organizations such as Human Rights Watch have documented many of these crimes. Government troops randomly shoot people, plunder, and set houses of suspects and their neighbors on fire. Attempts to weaken Boko Haram have ultimately made it stronger.

**Batula:** We then began to bury our dead. The dogs had already started to tear into them. We had to bury them. We couldn't just let the dogs devour them! There were five of us women who dared to go back into the village. I asked my aunt, sister of my mother, to look out for Boko Haram fighters so that she could warn us in time. We dug a hole for each of the dead. My arms hurt from all the digging. Among the dead we buried was also a soldier. We put sixteen people in the ground when the fighters suddenly appeared again. They were on motorcycles and on foot. They threatened to kill us. My aunt didn't see them. She was already very old. "Who told you that you are allowed to dig graves?" the Boko Haram men screamed at us. They hit and punched us. They tied our hands with plastic cords behind our backs and brought us into the house of the liquor merchant. Inside, they whipped us. I received thirty strokes. I will never forget this number. My whole back split open, my clothes soaked with blood. Even today my back hurts from these blows. My aunt who was supposed to have warned us about Boko Haram died a short while later. Boko Haram tied cloth around our heads so that we could not see anything. The whole night long we huddled with these cloths over our heads in that house. My old aunt died because the cloth wrapped around her head was too thick and she couldn't breathe properly. Her name was Cham. We heard how the whole night through she wheezed. "Loosen my cloth," she panted. But our hands were tied. She died at around four in the morning.

The next day, when the fighters returned, they saw she was dead. They threw my aunt into a well right in front of the house. I heard the sound of her body hitting the water. I was not able to cry at that moment. I was not able to think. The fighting continued. Suddenly around midday the military entered the village again. Our guards fled. A column of tanks. We'd heard them from far off. The scary creaking of their treads. The shots. One of us managed to untie herself, and then she freed all of us. We ran through the

village and for the mountains. We saw that soldiers had come
with five tanks. Boko Haram also had tanks, two tanks. They shot
at each other. We ran along the river as the military tried to cross
the bridge with its tanks. A Boko Haram tank fired and one of the
army's tanks plunged into the water. The Boko Haram fighters
had surrounded the military. Many of the soldiers now joined us
women and fled with us to the mountains. They begged us to
give them our clothes. They were so terrified that they wanted to
disguise themselves as women.

So again we saved ourselves in the mountains, twenty kilometers distant from Gubla, to the old kingdom of Sukur. But we were
not safe for long. Boko Haram hates the people of Sukur.

In the mountains above Gubla are the villages where people believe
in spirits—the "traditionalists," as anthropologists call them. The
inhabitants of the region around Sukur do not believe in Allah.
Officially, they are Christians, but in fact they believe in the existence of Zhigal (an omnipotent deity). They believe in Sakur-yum,
the rain god, in Piss, the sun god, in Maila, the god of the stars.
On the crests of hills and the summits of mountains they pray to
their gods at secret shrines, as they have for thousands of years.
UNESCO* designated Sukur a world heritage site in 1999. For
the people of Gubla, down by the river with their fertile fields,
the mountains represented a reservoir of cheap labor. For Boko
Haram, the people of Sukur are simply heathens. Like the Taliban
in Afghanistan and ISIS in Syria and Iraq, Boko Haram wants to
erase any pre-Islamic traces from its territory.

**Batula:** It took only a few days, and then Sukur was burning,
too. The fighters besieged the mountain. I found my husband in
Sukur again. He had fled there earlier. He was alive! I was so happy! For this time, the whole family was back together. We lived in

---

*The United Nations Educational, Scientific, and Cultural Organization the house of a friend, opposite the palace of Sukur, there, where earlier the Hidi, the most important chief of the community, had lived. When the Boko Haram fighters came, they set fire to the Hidi's palace. They burned all the settlements on the mountain to the ground. Such high flames! Everywhere fire and smoke. They shot at the men who tried to break through the circle of the siege. Boko Haram left only one narrow route open. They demanded we leave the village on this path or they would kill us. The surviving men who had surrendered were tied up. They had their upper arms bound so tightly that their chests stuck out. Then they were all loaded onto pickup trucks.

I still had enough time on the mountain to say good-bye to my husband. Just before he was taken away, he said, "How unjust life is. I cannot promise you I will survive this. Take care of the children." He held my hand. I just cried. I was not able to say anything to him. I couldn't speak.

**Rabi:** I said to Papa when we were separated, "I will pray for you. Please come back to me. I love you very much."

**Batula:** We never saw him again. I asked everyone I met in the next few months whether they'd seen him. But no one knew anything. I will never forget this sight: how he was thrown onto the back of the pickup truck. How he looked at me one last time. So much fear in his eyes.

The fighters took us women and the children down to Gubla. They did not say what they would do with us. There were about forty of us. Down in Gubla, at the big bus stop on the national road, I saw Babalaba, our neighbor. My mother is very good friends with his. He was now the leader of the Boko Haram fighters in this region. He saw me but pretended he did not know me. Next to him on the street kneeled sixteen men from our village. They kneeled in a long row. Babalaba said to us, "We have brought you here so that you will see how God's work is carried out."

Babalaba had earlier dealt in the skins of cows and goats. He is about thirty years old. He lives two houses from ours. I know he never looked after his family. He had a wife and three children. The roof of his house was leaky. The rain always went through. His family was poor. Before Boko Haram, he was a nobody. I don't know how he found his way to Boko Haram. He was often away from home. He always told us he had business in Cameroon. But early on there were rumors that he was with them, that he killed rich farmers in distant villages. After joining Boko Haram he changed. Suddenly he cared a lot about his family. He took care of his wife and brought them food and clothing. Babalaba never wore a mask. Everyone in Gubla knew who he was. He had eight scars on the left and eight on the right. When Boko Haram took the village, he kidnapped three girls and had someone marry them. Together with his family he took them and went into the forest.

They decapitated the men with long swords. They pushed a man down. One held the body firmly and another cut. It took a long time. I do not know how long. They then held the head high so that we could all see and threw it into the street. Then they dragged the next man out. These men had hidden inside houses and tried to flee the village. That's what we were told. Blood sprayed from the necks. The bodies quivered. Once the blood drains out, the body stops shaking. Before they had their heads cut off, their eyes were blindfolded. I knew all of the men. My oldest daughter's husband was among them. His name was Musa. Also kneeling in front of us were Haruna, Abdullah, Baba, Mai, Goro. I can also tell you the other names.

All were killed except for one: Ijakrayu. At first, he wanted to flee the village with the men, but then he turned against them. He worked with Boko Haram and showed them the path to a small, remote village. The village is called Wakara. Only Christians live there. Ijakrayu claimed he had once been a motorcycle driver in Lagos. But in the village he just hung around. He was lazy. He helped Boko Haram because he was afraid they'd kill him. I hear that eventually the military shot him.

That evening Babalaba and his men drove the young girls off in trucks. The same trucks came again the next morning. They forced us, the older women, onto the truck beds. I was taken away with my father. In the meantime we'd heard where they were taking us: into the Sambisa.

It is as though the Nigerian state is chasing its own shadow. With every operation that security forces carry out, the sect transforms itself, but never disappears. Society and the sect condition one another. It's not just terror that brings in new Boko Haram recruits. The state, as most Nigerians experience it in their daily lives, has little to offer. Democracy, extolled in the West as a miracle cure, has for a long time held no great hope. For many years, democracy has nourished an elite of fat-cat politicians. They belong to different parties but usually have the same goal: get rich fast. It is estimated that since independence in 1960 more than 400 billion dollars has been misappropriated.[1] The state's official laws serve to gauge the amount of bribe money paid, and these bribes, in turn, override the laws. Corruption follows only its own rules and cancels out any others. The most corrupt are the police and judges. The Nigerian plague that claims the most victims is not Boko Haram. It is rampant corruption.

Boko Haram is enticing because it promises to use Islamic law to reestablish a just society where all (Muslims) will be treated the same, regardless of wealth, social rank, or reputation. This is a deceptive hope. The Koran contains only a few fixed laws and many possible interpretations.

The army almost succeeded in capturing Abubakar Shekau in September 2012. He was near Maiduguri at a family party where a ceremony for a newborn was to take place. He escaped with a bullet wound to his thigh, but his wife and three children were arrested and have since then been detained. Shortly thereafter, Shekau recorded a video message. He seems quieter than usual, sitting in a brown tent with a Kalashnikov at his side. "Now that you have our women," he says, "Just wait and see what is in store for your women . . . your own wives, according to sharia law."

Rumor has it that Shekau fled to the Mali desert, to the city of Gao in the northeast. Here he is supposed to have nursed his injury for several months. Large swaths were overrun by Mali Islamic insurgents in the spring of 2012. Tuareg tribes that had fought for more independence allied themselves with a branch of al-Qaida called Ansar Dine (Defenders of the Faith). The Islamists in Mali seemed almost to have achieved their ultimate goal: an Islamic caliphate that would eventually spread over all of West Africa, from Gambia to Nigeria.

Different West African extremist groups grew together during the joint fighting in Mali. The military operations there led to an internationalization of Boko Haram's approach. It's not clear how many of its members fought on the side of Ansar Dine, but there are estimates that a hundred were stationed in Timbuktu alone. They made their headquarters in buildings belonging to customs authorities on the city's edge. They stayed there for about ten months, learning how to use automatic firearms and rocket-propelled grenades. The Boko headquarters were the French air force's first target when it attacked in January 2013, but by that point Shekau's fighters had already fled.

In March 2013 in a new video message, Shekau's wound seems to have healed. He had obviously returned to Nigeria. Now he threatened that in the next few months Boko Haram would start to kidnap people on a large scale.

Rabi has listened to her mother tell this story. She just looks at us, transfixed, especially me, probably the first white person she'd ever seen up close. After a while, she loses interest and plays around on her cell phone or watches the geckos. When she begins to speak, her voice is very quiet and halting, but in short order she speaks with more confidence and speaks faster, with the tone and rhythm many young girls here have: calm and steady.

**Rabi:** It was getting dark as we drove into the forest. So dark. I was afraid. I did not know what they'd done with my mother. They drove us deep into the forest and stopped under a large tree. That's where we spent the first night. The next morning the Chibok girls were brought to us. There were seven of them. Some fighters brought us water and cornmeal mash. The Chibok girls wore black burkas, so I could not see their faces. But their voices sounded very young. They said to us, "Why waste your time crying? When the fighters came and kidnapped us from our school in Chibok, we wanted to run. We jumped over the fence." Then they showed us the scars on their arms. "Don't worry," they told us. "You are here to carry out the work of God."

They said they lived with Shekau. In a camp, even deeper in the forest. People say Shekau had put a magic spell on the part of the forest where he lives to protect it. Anyone who sees where he lives without permission will never find his way back again. This is what the Chibok girls told us.

Then everything happened very fast. We had no time to think. That very same day we were married. All the girls they had just taken from Gubla.

The man they gave to me in the forest was called Mallam Umar. He was about twenty. He had joined Boko Haram when he himself was still very little. They had taken him from Maiduguri, where he was a student of the Koran. His mother is supposed to have died when he was still a child. That is what he told me. He wore a turban. He had a motorcycle and a gun.

He worked at a checkpoint at the entrance of the camp. He was often in a rage. He hit me. With a switch. The sort of switch that almost all teachers used in my old school. He hit me with it when

I said I wanted to go home to my mama. He did not like the food I cooked.

Rabi is silent and looks at the ground, fidgeting with her fingers. She cries without a sound. Tears run down her cheeks. She does not brush them off. Her mother lies next to her. She turns to her, but Rabi looks away.

**Batula:** I only know what she [Rabi] told me. He took her with him to Gulak. There he lived in an abandoned house whose owners had died or fled. They lived there for six months until the military took back the city. Then she returned with her husband to the forest.

Rabi interrupts her mother, sits up, and begins to tell her story again, this time with a firm voice. She does not call the fighter she was forced to marry "my husband." She calls him "the man."

**Rabi:** The worst were his friends. They were named Ibrahim and Moussa. They lived with us in the same house. When they were all together they always ordered me around and screamed at me. They threatened to beat me. For example, when I cooked something they didn't like. Or when I slept too long. Ibrahim and Moussa hit me a lot. It was the worst when Mallam Umar was not at home. Then they beat me most severely. His friends had also taken kidnapped women as wives. They lived with us in the same house.

Ibrahim's wife was older than I and came from Gwoza. Moussa's wife came from Michika, was Christian, and was about my age. They returned with us to the forest when the military appeared again. Ibrahim's wife fled on the same day as we did. Moussa's wife stayed in the Sambisa. Her mother was in the forest, and she did not want to leave her alone.

After Koran school, I cleaned the house, washed the dishes, and made the fire. The man usually came home at six o'clock with Moussa and Ibrahim.

In Gulak I once tried to run away. He left the house unlocked when they all went to the mosque. I ran away. But I did not make it far. A fighter stopped me. "Where are you going?" he wanted to know. "I am going home to my mother," I said. "Where is your home?" he wanted to know. "In Gubla," I said. He took me to a house with many women inside. I do not know how many there were anymore. They were being taught lessons from the Koran in order to be married later. They kept me for a week there, and then the man, along with Ibrahim and Moussa, came for me. I was terrified. I thought he would kill me. But he did not hit me. He led me from the building with the girls and then beat me at home. He beat me cruelly. With a stick. My back bled. My skin split open. He threatened to kill my mother if I ran away again.

He is an evil man. He should be beheaded. His head should be sliced off.

**Batula:** I did not know if Rabi was still alive until the morning the helicopters attacked our camp. I had the little ones with me—Zahra, Moussa, Alhaji, and Adamu. I did not know where the two older girls were. I begged the men to bring them to me once they had carried me off into the forest. But in the camp I saw my sister Sadiya! In the past, I had often traveled to Duhu to visit Sadiya. It takes one and a half hours by car to get to her village from mine. Now, in the forest, she lived under a tree only two hundred meters from mine.

Sadiya looked sick. She had malaria and a high fever. She had had been really sick four times in the past. The fever was so high that we thought she might have a miscarriage. Despite this, they forced her to go to Koran class every day. Then she often sat next to me. When we spoke to one another at the camp, we whispered.

The fighters had forbidden us from speaking Margi. They wanted to understand everything we said.

Her tree was taller than mine. It was warmer there. Our tree cast more shade because a lot of shrubbery grew close to its trunk. I asked the fighters if I could take my children to a different tree. They refused. There were so many snakes in the underbrush. Black snakes. Their heads were very small, but their bodies were as thick as my upper arm. They coiled through the branches. Fortunately, they never bit us. We often ran from this tree in panic because we saw a snake among its leaves. Then we waited. Sometimes the snake left by itself. When it stayed and we did not know where we should sleep, we asked a fighter for help. Then he'd shoot it. This happened two or three times a week.

Boko Haram divided the women in our camp into nine separate groups. They prohibited us from staying with the other women from Gubla. They mixed up the people of the different villages so that we would mistrust each other. Every group had its own section in the camp. Each one had guards and its own emir. Our emir was named Abu Muhommad, a Kanuri from Bama. Babalaba, my neighbor in Gubla, was in charge of all the groups. With his fighters, he now controlled the area from Gwoza down to Michika. Babalaba himself did not live with us in the camp. They said he lived with Shekau deep in the forest. There must have been about twenty boys watching us. Little boys, about fourteen or fifteen years old. The slightly older ones were given guns. The small ones got only machetes and axes. They threatened to use them but never did.

Many followers of Boko Haram are Kanuri, including Yusuf and Shekau. The Kanuri are the descendants of a people whose empire, the Kanem-Bornu Empire, once stretched from the oases of southern Libya to Cameroon. Their elites were the first to bring Islam to Nigeria in the eleventh century. The Kanuri resemble Arabs. They are usually tall and have a lighter complexion than other Nigerians. The Mai, the kings of the Kanem-Bornu Empire, traded with the Byzantine and, later, the Ottoman empires. They controlled the caravan routes through the central Sahara. Its fighters counted as the most feared of slave hunters. Humans were the most important commodities the Kanem-Bornu had. In the competitive struggle with other West African states, owning more slaves in Nigeria meant having more power. Slaves were the oil of West Africa. In the seventeenth and eighteenth centuries, their significance grew because rulers went to war with each other more often. To fund these conflicts they had to raise taxes on their subjects. This meant that farmers used slave labor on their plantations to a previously unknown degree because they did not want to fall into debt bondage.

The Kanem-Bornu Empire, later the Bornu Empire, lasted for more than a thousand years and disappeared only at the beginning of the twentieth century, when Germany, Great Britain, and France divided the territory among themselves. Still, also under colonial domination, the Kanuri managed to preserve their identity. For a long time they prevented the construction of schools and universities. For this reason, they are still suffering economically today. Their own inertia also put them at a disadvantage. The shehu* of Borno still lives in a palace in Maiduguri as the official descendant of Kanuri kings.

The second strongest group among the Boko Haram fighters is the Fulani. They, too, once had a powerful empire, the independent Sokoto Caliphate, which only in 1903 was conquered by the British. Only a small minority of Kanuri and Fulani support Boko Haram, but those who have joined the group hope for a return to the glory of earlier days.

**Batula:** You lose any sense of time in the camps. You don't know if a week or a month has passed. I think we were there for nine

---

*The title of the ruler of all Kanuris

months, but I am not sure. And then the bombs fell. Already a
few days before, bombers had attacked the "Gate 1" camp. After
that, Boko Haram brought the hostages to "Gate 2" because it
was deeper in the forest. Most of the fighters left for the front to
fight the army. When "Gate 2" was bombed, there were only a few
fighters there with the women and children.

The bombs started falling shortly after I woke up. I can remember three helicopters and two fighter jets. In all the confusion,
Rabi suddenly ran up to me. She had escaped her hut of plastic
sheeting, where she had to live with her husband, and searched
for me. So many people died all around us.

So many women and children. Some hid in the swamp's tall
grasses. Others sought cover behind trees. Splinters of wood
killed them. "Lie on the ground!" I said to my children. That is the
best thing you can do when bombs fall. We were shot at with artillery. This made a sound different from the bombs. First, you hear
a whistle, then the wood splinters. You hear the splitting wood,
then you hear the explosion. Everything on the ground burns.

Babalaba had warned us days ago that if we ever tried to flee
we would be slaughtered like sheep. I don't know what ever happened to him. The last time I saw him was the day before the
attack. He rode a big horse through our camp. His leg was bandaged. I knew the horse. It was a black and brown piebald from
the chief of Gubla. The chief would always ride this horse during
parades. A horse is precious for us. There were only four horses
in Gubla.

I was told that Babalaba escaped in the fire. I believe that
Babalaba, like Shekau, has magic powers. He can make himself
invisible and can shift from one place to another in seconds.

My sister Sadiya and I fled the camp on the same day, but she
went with a different group—with the women from Duhu. I ran
with the women from Gubla. Our groups ran in different directions.

Once we were outside the camp, I saw two children with burned skin. They belonged to a friend of mine. They were ten and fourteen years old, two boys. They were still alive and were lying on the ground. I tried to touch them, to take them with us, but I did not know where to hold them. There was no skin anymore! Oh my God, how they screamed. You should have heard how they screamed. Their mother stood next to me. "Mama!" they screamed. "Mama! Take us with you!"

Their mother left them behind. She had three other children with her. What should she have done? We ran through the burning camp. Bombs were still falling. The helicopter pilots shot at everything that moved. I saw so many dead. So many had died from the bombs. I saw my cousin's wife. She was named Gudine and was from Gubla. Her chest was split open.

I left my father behind. He could not stand up on his own. Before being abducted, he'd had an operation on his groin and had been in hospital for three months. Now, he was too weak to walk. When the air attack began, he tried to stand. But he fell down again. He tried again, and again his legs gave way. He broke into tears. I cried, too. "Father," I said to him. "We must go now, and I cannot carry you. Please forgive me. I have to go now." He said nothing. He just sat there and cried.

We ran in a direction we thought must be south. Our village was south of the Sambisa. There were thirty of us, women and children. We just crashed through the undergrowth. In the forest, you have to avoid the paths because otherwise you run into Boko Haram. I had five children with me. Rabi, Moussa (he is eleven), the seven-year-old Zahra, the four-year-old Alhaji, and Adamu—he is three. For five days we escaped through the forest. The afternoon of the first day we came to a large river. Its water was very dark. I took a stick and felt for bottom. It was too deep! We had children with us! We walked along its banks trying to find a crossing. But all along the banks grew bushes with thorns. Dreadful thorns with barbs. They are hard to get out of your skin. After a while, we were all bleeding. Even today, Rabi and I are covered with the scars of the wounds the thorns ripped into our flesh.

Eventually, we waded through the river. I held Zahra and Moussa by the hand. I had Alhaji on my back. Rabi carried Adamu and clung to my hijab. The water was up to my chest. It was so cold! I helped Rabi to stay above water. Once, I lost my balance and almost went under with my children, but I held on to a branch. The little ones swallowed water. They were so afraid.

It was crazy! I wish someone had recorded the scene on video!

She laughs.

**Rabi:** (*proudly*) I can swim. I can float, even when the water is deeper than I am tall. We had to cross many rivers, but this one was the deepest. In the middle of it a giant turtle swam to us. I was scared. I did not know if it would bite.

Nigeria's political parties obstruct each other in the fight against Boko Haram. The People's Democratic Party, to which former president Goodluck Jonathan belonged, and the biggest opposition group, the All Nigeria People's Party, which joined All Progressives Congress, the party of the current president, Muhammadu Buhari, accuse each other of having financed Boko Haram. Politicians from both parties have each other arrested. Most government parties in Nigeria are fueled not by politics but by business interests. Their names reflect a certain randomness: Fresh Democratic Party, Citizens Popular Party, African People's Alliance.

Not only the parties are entangled in various forms of patronage, but also the security forces. Security officers often feel more loyalty to local patronage networks than to the central state. In the past few years, ten generals from the North were convicted of passing attack plans along to Boko Haram.

In this war, Boko Haram is fighting a weakened military. In a country of 190 million inhabitants, the number of troops in the past few years has been reduced by more than half to just shy of eighty thousand. Since Nigeria achieved independence in 1960, the military has frequently organized coups against the government. Sani Abucha, the last soldier-president of Nigeria, died only in 1998 of a heart attack while in the company of three Indian prostitutes. Abucha had stolen 4.5 billion dollars from the state and had ruthlessly persecuted political opponents. For example, he had the writer and civil rights campaigner Ken Sarowiwa put to death in 1995. The parties that took power after Abucha's death tried to tame the military to prevent any further coups. Year after year, the government has reduced the military budget further to achieve this goal.

The condition of the police is similarly desperate. There are officially 330,000 police in Nigeria, but almost a third are occupied protecting high-ranking politicians and rich businesspeople who pay them bonuses on their salaries. The official average earnings of a police officer are 200 euros a month. At the end of 2014, the police force had to apply for credit. Mutinies threatened. The victims of a crime who wish to report it to the authorities have to be prepared to pay for the costs of the investigation, such as gasoline and hotel bills. Police often become hired thugs or sometimes even contract killers. Again and again, officers are accused of selling the identities of informants to Boko Haram.

The United States, for these reasons, has been reluctant to support Nigerian security forces for a long time. While it did help in the search for the kidnapped Chibok girls, Washington also pressured Israel not to provide the Goodluck Jonathan regime with combat helicopters. The United States again and again turned down requests for military aid. Only since the new president, Buhari, assumed power in 2015 has the government said it would try to fight corruption in the military and impose more discipline. The United States, in turn, altered its position slightly.

Nonetheless, the main burden in the battle against the terror sect is still carried by the neighboring states of Chad, Niger, and Cameroon.

**Batula:** On the second day of our escape we reached the swamps. Every step is an agony out there. The earth pulls at your feet. It holds on to you and does not let you go. One night, a scorpion stung my son Moussa. He screamed out loudly, and we were afraid Boko Haram would hear us. Moussa had two bites: one on his back and one on his scrotum. I had never seen such large scorpions. The first night we slept with our backs leaning against a tree trunk. The children lay on the ground around us. We could hardly sleep. So many insects! The little children were quickly covered in bites. There are also millipedes with stingers on their heads and their tails. Their bites are extremely painful.

On the afternoon of the second day, we saw a group of trees in the distance. Underneath the trees lay colorful blankets. We became afraid because we thought these belonged to Boko Haram fighters. They often climb trees to launch attacks from above. We sat and watched the trees for a long time. But nothing moved. We cautiously moved closer, and then we saw the corpses. I cannot say anymore how many there were. Most were women. Maybe they starved to death while escaping. I saw a woman from Gubla. She lay on her stomach as though sleeping. I thought she was still alive. I knelt down and touched her. Her body was cold. It was Ama. She used to sell bean cakes at our market. She was an elderly lady. She came into the world with a disability. She limped. She loved children. All children wanted to buy things from her because she'd give them a cake for free.

**Rabi:** As we were running away, I was afraid all the time that the man would find me—the man they gave to me in the forest. He had threatened to kill me if I took off. I saw how he killed people. He was there when five hostages were executed. Three men and two women. They were accused of committing adultery. The fighters buried them to the neck in the ground and then threw stones at their heads. They blindfolded the men, not the two women. The women died quickly. The men took longer. The top of the skull of one of them burst open and you could see the brain.

Another time they kidnapped ten Christians from Michika. They shot two. The other eight had their heads cut off in front of all of us. The man[*] tied their hands together and bound cloth over their eyes. I saw how he cut off the heads of two of them. He was sweating and very upset when he returned to our sleeping place. This was a sort of room made from black plastic sheeting. "I will do the same thing to you if you run away again," he said. This night he forced himself on me. He said he was carrying out the will of almighty God.

**Batula:** We always took our direction from the sun. That is how we found a way out of the forest. On the fourth day the swamps became drier and the trees sparser. When we reached the edge of the forest, the first thing we did was search for water. We were so thirsty. That's when we came across the hole. It was actually not a hole at all but a broad hollow. It was full of dead bodies. Most of them were men. Not only a few or a dozen. There must have been about a hundred. I don't know who killed them or who they even were.

**Rabi:** We walked along paths and small trails through the savannah until finally we reached a village, where we met the army. The soldiers drove us in trucks back to Gubla, our village. But we couldn't stay there. They had burned down most of the churches and houses. Many had collapsed. A tank had destroyed the big mosque. Even our house was just a charred ruin. All our photographs were gone. They always do that. They do not like photos.

---

Her husband

I saw how they set a big pile of photos on fire in front of the big church in Gubla. They had also burned my clothing. The roof had a huge hole in it. We covered it with plastic sheeting and then left for Gulak, where my aunt lives.

A few days later my mother bore a child. It is a boy. He is named Kabir, and he has funny ears.

**Batula:** Our village was not only destroyed by Boko Haram. While they ravaged much of it, other people caused most of the damages. Tanks shot up the big mosque. The minaret was hit and fell to the street. I heard that soldiers drove their vehicles into the mosque walls on purpose to get revenge. The people of Sukur brought about the most damage. They set fire to Gubla. They shot dead all the men they saw. They killed up to seventy of our men. They sent their women and children into the valley to loot our abandoned houses. They stole twenty-three sacks of corn from me! I've heard that at some point their chief called them back. Now our men guard the village. They established a militia. They are armed with bows and arrows, but they are there only during the day. And even they are thieves and robbers. They have stolen much of what Boko Haram left behind. Long before the sun goes down they leave the village and drive back to Gulak. No one lives in our village anymore, not even thieves. At night Boko Haram comes from the bush.

The areas the abductees return to are in many parts not habitable anymore. Boko Haram has in many places been known to throw corpses into wells. When they withdraw from an area, they blow up the bridges, so that now, during the rainy season, whole regions are isolated for months because the rivers are impassable. Amnesty International has been able to document the enormous extent of the destruction with the help of satellite imagery.

Boko Haram not only destroys buildings. It also shreds the very fabric of society. No region in the world is so rich in distinct languages and ethnicities. Their relationships to one another are historically complicated and fragile. Boko Haram has confounded the delicate balance. Countless local revenge campaigns rage in northeastern Nigeria. Hundreds of people die in their wake.

The people of Sukur are carrying out a terrifying revenge against Gubla because they, too, have experienced great suffering. Even more than the Christians, the leaders of Boko Haram detest animists. Sukur is one of the last strongholds of animism in Nigeria. For centuries, every family here has been responsible for a specific shrine.

After taking the valley in the summer of 2014, hundreds of Boko Haram fighters headed for the surrounding mountains where animists dwell. Sukur's chief reported that the fighters torched shrines and fetishes. "Any Muslim who, uninvited," he explains, "crosses our territorial boundaries will be killed." Nevertheless, Boko Haram found supporters among Sukur's young, who betrayed the secrets of the elders. The fighters forced the priests to take them to shrines and they destroyed them. The people of Sukur number about ten thousand according to the chief. Boko Haram has killed between three hundred and four hundred of them. He said that about 40 percent of the population has been abducted. Most have been taken to the Sambisa.

"They say our traditions go against Islam," the chief told me. "Sukur is not the same anymore. The soul of this place has been destroyed." Once Boko Haram had withdrawn, 150 of Sukur's young men were executed, 150 men who, under Boko Haram's influence or by force, had converted to Islam. "We had to kill them." He admits that Sukur's militias sacked Gubla but also points out that many Gubla residents participated. He mentions Babalaba, Batula's former neighbor.

Death came to Sukur from Gubla, says the chief.

UNESCO learned about the destruction of the Sukur shrines from our research. The Paris headquarters of UNESCO are also very far away from northeastern Nigeria.

**Batula:** They burned Babalaba's house down out of revenge. He took his parents with him to the forest. We heard his father died there. He'd always had high blood pressure. The men of Sukur hated Babalaba, and they knew he came from Gubla. And they also knew that many young men in Gubla had joined Boko Haram. Many of the bad people in Gubla. The blacksmiths, for example. They all come from slaves. We don't think much of them. We don't eat what the blacksmiths cook. This can bring bad luck. Blacksmiths are not good people. Never would I allow my daughter to marry a blacksmith! And many of our blacksmiths joined Boko Haram.

We now live with my aunt in Gulak, but even in Gulak it is not safe. A week ago, Boko Haram men stabbed seven of my relatives at night—in their sleep. I am very afraid that they will also want to take revenge against me. But I don't know where I should go. I miss the people who are still in the forest. My husband is still in the Sambisa, and my second-oldest daughter, Adda, too. I do not know if they are still alive or dead. What does God have in store for them?

Adda should actually have married by now. The wedding had been planned for around this time. A boy from the village fell for her. He worked at the clinic in Gubla and was responsible for the medicine cabinet. He is about twenty, a boy from the neighborhood. His name is Iddi. Already two years before Boko Haram came to the region, he had proposed to her. The negotiations between our families were successfully ended. We had all agreed that the wedding should happen only once Adda had finished high school. So, this year. He was to have paid a 40,000 naira (*about 180 euros*) dowry. That is a good price for us in Gubla. He also wanted to add five boxes of clothes, cosmetics, underwear, and earrings. Iddi's father was the chairman of the farmers' association. They're a good lot. I hear now that Iddi has fled to Yola.

**Rabi:** I want to marry only in five years, once I have finished school. The man I marry must respect my mother. He should not scream or hit me. He should be a little funny. And gentlemanly.

**Batula:** I did not meet my daughter Adda even once in the forest. I heard she is in a camp deep in the Sambisa. She is very sensitive, sometimes also difficult. You have to tell her everything twice. Rabi has more friends and has more visitors than Adda. She also does better in school. Adda is a shy girl. She was always very quiet.

I fled the Sambisa, but I still think often about that forest. Shekau put a spell on us. That's what they told us in the forest. "Shekau will find you wherever you are." When it is quiet all around me, very still, and no one speaks or wants anything from me, then I am once again in the forest.

"You will now really understand the person called Shekau. You don't know my madness, right? It is now that you will see the true face of my madness. I swear by Allah's holy name that I will slaughter you. I will not be happy if I don't personally put my knife on your necks and slit your throats. Yes! I'll slaughter you! I'll slaughter you! And I'll slaughter you again and again."

—Abubakar Shekau, April 2014

# THE CAVE

The house in Yola where we meet Sakinah makes us feel uneasy. It is a building between two major roads. Now and then vehicles stop behind the entrance gate. Men now and then stand in front of the house with their cell phones. Sometimes they look out at the street, sometimes up at us. Our interpreter had thought this would be a good place to meet. We are in the offices of the Islamic Council. The administration handed over the building to the translator for two days. He had told no one that foreign reporters were coming. No one else is on the premises. We did not want to interview thirty-three-year-old Sakinah in a Christian parish because she is Muslim. In the tense atmosphere in Yola, we did not want to make any mistakes. But now we don't feel comfortable in this building. Perhaps, however, we are just being too anxious. We close all windows and doors for the next few hours to prevent anyone from looking in. Our driver waits in the car in the forecourt, listening to the radio for news of the latest bomb attacks and looking out for anything suspicious.

Sakinah comes with her twenty-three-year-old cousin Isa. He works as a goat trader in Gulak. He also plays in the village soccer club as forward for a team called Sanussi United. At first, we sit on a rug, but after a few hours we lie down. Isa is a shy and lanky young man who often laughs awkwardly. Sakinah is a self-confident worker. She is a traditional birth attendant in her village, a respectable occupation. Birth attendants often substitute for the midwife and even the doctor. They are admired but also feared at times. She is a wise woman and is careful in what she says.

**Sakinah:** I used to think I was a strong woman, but I was wrong. Once you've been abducted by Boko Haram, you'll never be normal again.

I live in a village that is not far from Gulak. My father was a soldier and constantly being transferred, so we moved around the country. I was born in Sokoto, in the northwest. When I was eight, we moved to Lagos, all the way in the South. He died when I was eleven. After his death, we moved to my mother's village, here near Gulak. That was a big adjustment. I missed Lagos, the big city, very much. My friends were there in Lagos. The food is different here in the village. The fish, the vegetables—everything tastes different. In the village, you have to work hard on the fields to have just enough to cook something. In the city you just go to the fridge, and it's got everything you want. In Lagos, our mother ran a store in a military barracks that sold soft drinks. We had our own refrigerator there. Now, in this village we don't even have electricity.

I went to high school in Gulak, but then my mother fell ill and I had to take care of her. I quit school in the seventh grade. Mother suddenly had a high fever, and for the next two years after that she wasn't able to walk. She just lay in her room. Some said it was a curse. I think she suffered from depression. Like me, she also longed for the big city. I had to feed her and wash her. I had to wash her clothes. At some point, the state stopped paying us a survivor's pension. That was a difficult time.

My father had four wives. My mother was the second. Of the other three, two died. One died of an illness. The other one was killed by Boko Haram. She locked herself in her house when the fighters came. They just shot through the door and she was dead. Only two days later was the corpse found.

I married when I was eighteen. I chose my husband myself, even though I was so young. I met him for the first time when I went to the market in Madagali to sell the beans that my mother grew. That's where I met him—when he bought beans from me.

His name is Yakubu. He is a goat dealer. I did not know exactly how old he was, but a lot older than I. It was not love at first sight. I discovered my love for him only later. He was always smartly dressed and had a neat appearance. He smiled a lot. My parents made inquiries about him and his family in the city and received only good news. He had gone to school in Mubi and then built up his goat business from scratch. We married on January 7, 2000. Eventually, I moved in with his family, ten kilometers from Gulak. We had six children. They are: Idrissa, eleven years old, Garba, nine, Moussa, seven, Suleman, five, Rukayya, who died when he was five, and Omar, who is two.

The eldest, Idrissa, died fleeing from Boko Haram. I learned this only after I had escaped. She had already been sick before the raid. She had a fever, and we were not able to have her treated. The government had imposed a curfew. The hospitals had shut down a long time before.

After our wedding, I got my own piece of land. I'd asked him for it so I could grow peanuts and red beans. Red beans sell for a higher price than white beans or chad beans. Also, you need to use pesticides to grow chad beans. They are more sensitive than other beans. In our village, the day begins very early. I wake up at five, pray, and then shell peanuts. Then I take them to the mill and have them ground. I cook the mash and strain the oil from it. With the rest I bake small cakes. We call them kulikuli. At the same time, I make food for the children and send them off to school. This all has to happen before six in the morning. At about two o'clock in the afternoon I am finished with the peanut cake. I sweep the house and wash the dishes. The children come home from school and we eat. After five o'clock, I sit with other women in front of my house and we talk, usually until the sun goes down.

When it gets dark outside, I help the children at home with their homework as much as I can. Often I cannot help them because I left school at such an early age. My son Moussa always needs the most help. He is good at grammar, but reading out loud for him is very difficult. He finds it hard to focus. He is aggressive and beats up other children. I slap him sometimes because I cannot control him any other way. I don't hit him hard, only enough to make him remember.

The happiest moment of the day for me is the evening, when I can finally lie down, when everything is quiet in the house. The stillness and the tiredness—so good together.

In the spring of 2014, Boko Haram transformed itself once again. The Nigerian political establishment was busy preparing for the World Economic Forum for Africa in Abuja. This prestige project was meant to attract investors to Nigeria. The government was not paying much attention to what was happening in the north of the country. Boko Haram, which had started out as a peaceful group of people seeking spiritual meaning and then later turned into a jihadist guerrilla unit, mutated once again into a more or less conventional army. The various command units merged and became one organism.

The Islamic sect no longer hid or retreated. Until this time, Boko Haram had always quickly fallen back after an attack. Now, the fighters increasingly held on to captured territory. On August 6, 2014, they advanced out of the Sambisa for Gwoza, which Shekau immediately proclaimed would be the capital of the Islamic caliphate. A bit later, they occupied Bama, a town about sixty kilometers away. They conquered almost the entire north of the country along the borders with Chad and Niger. At the same time, they attacked neighboring Cameroon deep into the country and extending their territory almost exactly to the border of the old Kanuri Kanem-Bornu Empire. They kidnapped the wife of Cameroon's deputy prime minister, freeing her months later in exchange for a ransom in the millions. On August 23, the fighters attacked Madagali in the neighboring state of Adamawa. In early September, they advanced on Gulak, and soon after they overran the predominantly Christian Michika. By the end of October, Mubi, a metropolis of 200,000 inhabitants, fell. In November, they were just one hundred kilometers from Yola. Just six months after their offensive began, the Boko Haram fighters had conquered nearly the entire Kanuri tribal homeland. They now ruled a territory the size of Belgium, with a population of 2 million.

**Sakinah:** The best job in the village is being a tailor. There are only four in our village. I have tried to save for a few years to afford a sewing machine. They cost one hundred dollars. Still, hardly do I put some money away than I had a new problem. My mother's illness. I lent my brother money. He is lazy and doesn't get much out of his fields, but he has a lot of children—eight children. His wife, who earns her own money, and I pay his children's school fees!

I heard about Boko Haram for the first time about six years ago, when I was in Maiduguri for a wedding. I was pregnant at the time, with Suleman. My cousin was getting married. We were in the city on the day the preacher Yusuf was killed. The celebration had to be cut short, and we had to run. In the city I heard men from Boko Haram scream, "We will destroy Maiduguri!" On the way back to my village I saw corpses on the street for the first time.

They attacked my village about a year ago. It was a Friday in September 2014. Just the previous day I had baked kulikuli cakes. During these weeks school had been canceled. A curfew had been in force for three weeks. But no one expected Boko Haram to come so soon. Yakubu, my husband, was at home teaching the Koran to our children. We had a wooden tablet they could write on. Every child had a tablet. Boko Haram took those. When they attacked, it was pouring rain. I had washed the children's clothes. We had just made a fire for our evening meal.

Then we heard shots very close to the mosque, about a hundred meters from us. I had spread the clothes out to dry in the courtyard because it had finally stopped raining. I threw myself on the ground. The children ran for cover. My husband got a shovel to make a hole in the far wall of the courtyard. He and Isa hacked their way through and left me behind. I was not angry at them. We all knew what Boko Haram does to the men it captures. They shoot them dead. They just kidnap us women.

Isa speaks with a soft voice. Our interpreter has to lean in close to hear him. Sakinah calls Isa the "cat with seven lives."

**Isa:** I ran with Sakinah's husband. A friend of mine was a few meters ahead of us. His name was Tappalira. As he burst through the door onto the street, a bullet instantly hit him. Tappalira was dead. There was no means of escape for us anymore. So Sakinah's husband and I turned around and made a hole through the wall of the backyard. Luckily, it was the rainy season, so the wall was very soft. If it had been the dry season, we would not have managed it. We ran, leaping over five walls. In our village, every field is surrounded by walls. They chased us first in a pickup truck, a Toyota Hilux, but then they came on foot because the roads were too narrow for their vehicles. They ran after us. They just would not quit. For an hour and a half they chased us. Sometimes we hid to shake them off. We waited a half hour in hiding and then began to run again. As we were climbing the sixth wall, they spotted us again. They shot. They hit Sakinah's husband in the leg. From that point on I had to carry him. I hauled him through tall, thick grass. That's where I bandaged his wound. He'd been struck in the knee and it bled a lot. I put a flat stone between his teeth so that he could bite down if the pain became too much, so he would not scream too loudly. It was dark when we reached the mountains. Boko Haram had captured my father as he was climbing over a village wall. They cut off his head with a chain saw.

**Sakinah:** I was so disoriented. I ran inside the house, crouched down, and prayed. Prayed for the men to survive their escape. My mother-in-law was with me. When it grew dark, I went outside to look for my children and my husband. I was very afraid, but I had to do something. I prowled through the cornfields.

**Isa:** The traditional hideouts for people from our village are in the mountains. There are three big caves there. One of them is many kilometers long. It's an old shrine. It is beautiful. Nowhere else do you see such beauty. The walls inside this cave have many different colors.

After about an hour walking inside the cave you reach an underground stream with good, fresh water. Every April, people from the villages of our area come to this cave for a ceremony. We call it Dukkwa. People leave offerings up there. We slaughter goats there so that Yalikda* protects our villages. Many can see his spirit during the ritual. His shrine is in the cave. Until now I have only seen him once. Yalikda decides who he'll show himself to and in what form. He appeared to some of my friends as an old woman, to others as a monkey. He appeared to me in the cave as a snake with two horns on its head. We fled to this cave.

**Sakinah:** After four hours, I reached the cave in the mountains. I was all alone. It was dark, and I had no flashlight when I arrived at the entrance. I could see no faces. I only heard the voices. I asked after my children, but the voices said there were no toddlers in the cave. Only bigger children. The small ones, they said, were not allowed there because their cries might give away the hideout.

Boko Haram's organization remains unclear, though it has existed for five years. It's still not known who makes the decisions. The following sketch is based on speculation from Nigerian security experts. Boko Haram is composed of six major factions. The leader of one of these groups accuses Shekau of giving the Kanuri, members of his own tribe, too much power. The most important

---

*The most supreme god of the Margi

of the splinter groups calls itself Ansaru, or "Jama'atu Ansarul Muslimina fi Biladis Sudan," which means "Vanguard for the Protection of Muslims in Black Lands." It allegedly broke away from Boko Haram in 2012. The Ansaru faction criticized Shekau because they said that under his command too many innocent Muslims had been killed. Ansaru has better connections with terror groups in the Sahel and is supposed to have specialized in kidnapping foreigners. This group is accused of abducting German civil engineer Edgar Raupach in 2012. The splinter groups work sometimes loosely, sometimes closely, together, but in general they need to rely on one another. They are supposed to share ransom money, but this also sometimes leads to conflict.

Shekau's position as Boko Haram's leader is merely symbolic. His title is *amir ul-Aam* (supreme emir). Beneath him are two deputies. They are the only ones allowed to discuss matters of strategy with him. Lower-tier commanders are not allowed to contact Shekau directly. Major decisions are made by the *shura*, the council of commanders (depending on the source, this council has between seven and thirty members). Each commander is in charge of a *lajna* (sector) of Boko Haram. In the Hausa language, these commanders are called *kwamandoji*. The *shura* is meant to embrace members of the splinter groups. *Kwamandoji* deputies, known as *munzirs* (herald), lead Boko Haram foot soldiers, the *maaskars*. Boko Haram has departments for their intelligence service, for fund-raising, for the planning of suicide attacks, for the procurement of guns and vehicles, and for the planning of military operations.

Certain *shura* members see to the payment of fighters, to the financial support of those they leave behind, and to the administration of a kind of health insurance plan. This provides members with free health care. In this regard, Boko Haram fighters enjoy a higher standard of living than members of the Nigerian army.

This structure replicates itself at the local level. To what extent local cells coordinate is not clear. There is method in their madness.

**Sakinah:** That first night I slept near to the cave under a tree. With me were about a hundred other refugees. Early in the morning I met a woman who said another village woman had fled with my children. During the next few days, I went again and again to the mouth of the cave and asked after my husband, but no one knew anything.

After sundown on the second day I sneaked back into the valley [which was still controlled by Boko Haram], to our house, where I found my mother-in-law. She hugged me and cried. She also had no idea where my children and husband were.

**Isa:** We stayed in the cave for four days. The cave is called Duhu. We left it only at night. We had no cell phone reception. Boko Haram had blown up all the cell towers in the area. At the end of the fourth day our guard saw a Boko Haram detachment. They were coming up the mountain on foot. There were many of them. I've heard that a spy in our village told them about our cave. We all ran away. We ran as fast as we could. They killed two of us. They shot at us from a distance. Only the darkness saved us. We decided to cross the border to flee into Cameroon. The plan was to creep back down into the valley and from there back into the mountains. Then, at some point we'd reach Cameroon.

We men divided ourselves into three groups. One group was in charge of defense. In case of an attack, they were to throw stones at the Boko Haram fighters. The second group was in charge of fetching water. The men of the third group helped the women. We had about fifty women with us. Two of us supported Sakinah's husband. So we fled over the mountains to Cameroon. It took us two weeks.

**Sakinah:** After looking in the fields, I looked for my children on the main road. I couldn't find any leads. Still no one knew anything. When I closed my eyes at night, I saw my children. I went to my brother's house. Like all the other men, he'd run away a long time ago. My children were not there either. My brother's pregnant wife lay on a mat on the floor. My mother, that is, her mother-in-law, sat next to her. She was having bad labor pains. "Please stay," she said to me. "If I die while giving birth and the child survives, take the child and raise it." I hid up in the mountains for a month and came down to the village to take care of my sister-in-law. Boko Haram is not on the move at night or when it rains. At those times you are safe.

My sister-in-law was anemic. The pregnancy had wiped her out. In the mountains, I gathered the bark of a special tree. It is called idirmashi. I cut it off the trunk. I cooked up a brew from it that makes pregnant women's blood thicker. It seemed to help. The swelling in her legs went down.

Every evening, I snuck down into the village. I clambered down into the valley until I reached a boulder, very close to the first houses. I hid behind it. I waited for darkness to fall, and, if I didn't hear any noise from a motor for a while, I'd keep going and cross the A13. The best time to enter the village was at about six o'clock, when they were all in the mosque for evening prayer. At about midnight I'd leave the village again. I'd put my veil on and pretend to be a Boko Haram wife. My plan was to escape after the birth with my mother, my sister-in-law, and the child.

To stop Boko Haram, Nigeria's government entered into a pact with self-defense groups that would lead only to more bloodshed. Although ever more reinforcements were sent to the North, the military and the police failed in their fight against Boko Haram. Even elite troops from Chad and Cameroon were not able to change the situation.

So in its battle with the devil, the government created another one. It formed civilian defense groups, the so-called Civilian Joint Task Forces, or CJTF. The first of them were formed in Maiduguri, Boko Haram's most coveted prize. The new militias were composed of young men from the city's neighborhoods who just wanted to protect their families. But there were also criminals in the mix. Unintentionally, the state had hired gang members, who were accustomed to making the streets dangerous, to ensure its own security. The new militias set up checkpoints and actually patrolled the streets, whereas the military had entrenched itself safely in its bases. The defense leagues spread throughout the northeast. The solution to countering Boko Haram seemed finally to have been found.

Goodluck Jonathan, Nigeria's former president, referred to members of the militias as "national heroes." He put them under the command of the Nigerian military. They were allocated numbered sectors of territory to patrol and were given badges and guns. Quickly, however, they became the people's new scourge. These militias have by now gained a reputation for randomly killing and plundering. Thousands of people, without trial, have reportedly been killed. Militia members have been accused of rape. They also intensify the tension between tribes. Every tribe now has its own militia, sometimes even two, which then compete with one another over resources.

Armed with machetes and old hunting rifles, they stand at their checkpoints, demanding money from anyone who wishes to pass. They are dressed in rags and their eyes are red. Many of these "national heroes" are drunk or on drugs. In most of the villages from which Boko Haram has been driven these are the new masters. The Nigerian military rarely operates outside the big cities. The militias look like they belong in a Mad Max film, but they are the only alternative to Boko Haram. Nonetheless, it is hard to say which group is more brutal.

**Sakinah:** My sister-in-law had twins. We had no idea she was pregnant with twins! She delivered the first baby, but the second one remained inside her. That's when I decided to stay with her full time. The second, undelivered child threatened her life. She threw up a lot and had foam on her lips. Then she lost consciousness. When we saw a Boko Haram vehicle drive by, my mother ran out to flag it down. What else could we do? She asked for help. They came back half an hour later with a nurse. We told the fighters that my brother, the new mother's husband, was one of them and that he would fight for them. I also told them that my husband was Boko Haram and that he'd be returning in a few days. The nurse was not from here. She did not speak Hausa. A Boko Haram fighter translated for her. Her skin was as white as an Arabian's. When she worked she always wore plastic gloves. She wore a burka but took it off for the birth. She gave my sister-in-law an intravenous drip and medicine. She said she works in a Boko Haram clinic in Gwoza. My sister-in-law brought a girl and a boy into the world.

On the sixth day after the birth, Boko Haram was at our door again. They asked me, "Is your husband back?" I lied to them again. They asked me, "What team is he with" I didn't have an answer for that, so they took me with them. If only they'd returned a bit later! I had wanted to flee with my sister-in-law the next day. Before that she had simply been too weak.

One held me by the wrist, another pushed me toward a pickup truck, and a third was at my side holding a gun. I had to leave my sister-in-law and mother behind. The Boko Haram men forced me onto the bed of the pickup. They took me to Madagali and then to Gwoza, where they locked me in a house with many other captured women.

On the first day, I counted twenty women. On the second, there were already fifty, with many children. We were Muslim and Christian, but there were more Christians. We had no Koran lessons. I stayed there for the next two weeks.

Every morning, a fighter picked me up and drove me to a house where another fighter had moved in. I had to do the washing and help his wife. The fighter had kidnapped her in Mubi. Poor girl, she cried every day. I tried to console her, but what consolation could I give? She would escape if she were able, she told me. She could not have been older than fourteen. The man she was given to as wife was no older than twenty. He was a little guy. He didn't have a beard yet. He had seen her in Mubi, thought she was pretty, and told his father he wanted to marry her. But the father countered that he should be patient, the girl was still too young. So the lad shot both her parents—in front of her eyes. That's how she told it to me. He paid her a five-thousand-naira dowry and took her with him. I le raped her constantly. He forced her to sleep in his bed. I heard her praying often that soldiers should come and kill her husband.

Sometimes he called to her, and if she refused to come he held a gun barrel to her head. That's when I was paralyzed with fear. I stayed quiet. I never said anything. I still think a lot about her. Should I have said something? Will God punish me one day because I didn't help her? He screamed at the girl, "I will kill you! The same way I killed your parents!" He was a Kanuri and spoke Hausa badly. The girl was not able to escape. An old man was always in front of the house, watching her.

Her name was Raheema, and she was a Muslim. At some point, her husband took her away on a motorcycle.

One day they hustled us out of the house and said they were taking us to the Sambisa. But this time there were no trucks. We went on foot, a long line of women and children and Boko Haram fighters. At first they let us walk on the streets, but then jets flew overhead and they forced us into the bush. Every time jets appeared, the fighters would mix in with us. If we die, they said, we die together. We had about sixty children with us. They said they wanted to take the children into the Sambisa the better to teach them Islam. "If your men don't come for you in a year," they said to the women who pretended they were already married, "we will marry you off." They are liars! They would have murdered my husband had he come for me. They are liars!

We women, we walked at the very front of the line, the children at the end. Some of the fighters drove ahead with their motorcycles and then came back. They checked to find out if the route was safe. However, most of the fighters were on foot, like us. There were about fifty men. They walked in the middle of the column between the children and us. We were not allowed to rest. It was hot. At some point, I really thought I would not survive the march. The children suffered the most. During the two days we walked, some children died. They couldn't walk anymore. Already before the march, these children were undernourished. Three died: one was six, one four, the other eight.

If a child collapsed at the end of the line, an older one called for help. But the fighters did not allow us to stop. The children whined. They begged for water, for food. The fighters threatened to shoot them if they complained. Some of the women had been kidnapped with their children, who were also with us in this column. Sometimes they turned and looked behind them, and sometimes their children ran to the front of the line to be with their mothers, but the fighters ripped them from their mothers and carried them to the back of the line.

As we walked through the bush, we all ate the fruit that grew on our route. I tripped three times. The sun burned. I was dizzy. They gave us nothing to eat. Also no water. No one helped me to get up. We were all on our own. No one helped anyone else. "Hurry up!" the fighters screamed. They screamed that a thousand times. "Hurry up! Move it!"

At this time, I also saw two white men. They helped Boko Haram. Their job was to repair the vehicles and fix the heavy weaponry. I often saw them standing with tools at one of the tanks. They worked on five tanks. They spoke no Hausa, but they did speak good English. One of them looked like you.

She looks at me. I am only the second white person she has seen up close. She tells me now that she was afraid of me when we first met for our conversation because I resembled the other white man. Many Muslim Europeans have joined ISIS in Syria and Iraq. A few white jihadists have also been spotted in Mali fighting for Ansar Dine. Until now, it wasn't known that Boko Haram had white fighters. Nigeria seemed too distant, Boko Haram too isolated. However, Boko Haram's military successes and the founding of the caliphate changed that.

Boko Haram has now allied itself with ISIS, as have most of the other West African terrorist organizations. Though Boko Haram had sworn allegiance to al-Qaida, it broke with that organization in 2014. The success of ISIS in Syria and Iraq deeply impressed the leaders of Boko Haram. It is also probably no coincidence that Shekau began his conquering campaign just one month after the proclamation of an ISIS caliphate in Mosul, Iraq, in June 2014.

In the summer of 2014, representatives of Boko Haram reportedly met in Mecca with leaders of ISIS, al-Shabaab, from Somalia, al-Qaida in the Islamic Maghreb (AQMI), from Algeria, and Ansar Dine, based in northern Mali. The ISIS emissaries pressured Boko Haram to change its tactics. That is, Boko Haram was told to stop ransacking villages and then withdrawing. Rather, the new strategy called for retaining the territory. Apparently ISIS promised to support Shekau with weaponry and volunteers. At the same time, ISIS trained Boko Haram fighters.

Hundreds of Boko Haram members have fought in the Syrian, Iraqi, and Libyan conflict zones. Those who survive return as specialists in bomb construction and military tactics. The attack strategies of many Boko Haram operations now resemble those of ISIS in Iraq. Small and mobile units attack quickly and move on. Even Boko Haram videos, which previously resembled those of al-Qaida, now look more like the sophisticated videos sent from ISIS.

In September 2014, a small ISIS delegation, with members from the Sudan, Syria, and Libya, reportedly visited the newly declared Boko Haram caliphate. Hundreds of Arab specialists traveled to

Borno in order to give Boko Haram logistical support, according to security experts.

**Sakinah:** They weren't Arabs, and they weren't from here. They were as white as you. One of them wore a djellaba, the other a black leather jacket. They did not walk with us in the long line. I saw them at different places. Always repairing vehicles. We also saw them again in Bita, a village on the edge of the Sambisa.

The people of Bita had all fled. When we arrived, the village was practically empty. Almost all the stores at the market had been broken into. Only the fighters and their families were there. We were separated from the children in Bita. We were again locked up in a house. They took the children somewhere else. Maybe to the forest. They cried. The men screamed. Then the door closed shut. I don't know what they did with the children.

The door opened only when they gave us food. They explained nothing. We had no idea what they wanted to do with us. On the second day, we heard a lot of pickup trucks come into the village, along with a lot of fighters. The guard at our door, the one who always gave us our food, told us that Shekau would be arriving that night. "The sultan of all Muslims is near," he told us. Come evening we heard the guards in front of our house break into song. They sang, "We await the son of Mohammed Yusuf!" The next morning the guard came again to us and said that Shekau had been here. The guard told us Shekau was not happy that his fighters had kidnapped so many women and children from the villages and cities. Shekau said that Boko Haram was at war and they should concentrate on fighting. "Are you going to let us go?" I asked. "We will not let you go," the guard said.

The door to our room was always locked, except for when jets flew over the village. That's when they let us out and herded us onto a meadow in front of the house. They did not want the jets to attack. The men ran up to us and hid among us. They forced us out into the open. We did not want to go. We were afraid.

But then the jet did attack, though we all stood on the meadow. It was the evening of the fourth day. Everywhere burning trees. We ran away through the confusion. Five of us. My younger sister is still with Boko Haram. She was too weak to come with us. I don't know what happened to her.

**Isa:** We men fled deeper and deeper into the bush. After Boko Haram had discovered the cave we ran. For the next two months, we stayed there in the bush. We could go nowhere else. In the villages all around, Boko Haram had men. As we escaped, we buried Idrissa, Sakinah's older daughter. We had no medicine. We ate only raw corn in the mountains, drank creek water. The water made Idrissa sick. She had diarrhea. She threw up a lot. She was constantly retching. For three days she vomited. Until she was dead. She cried a lot, saying, "I am sick, and my mama is not here." I tried to comfort her. "Your mama will come. Stay alive until she gets here." Before the attack, Idrissa was in the seventh grade. We buried her in the garden of a deserted house in the village of Lassa. We made an oval out of stone over her grave.

**Sakinah:** We now live together in Yola, in an unfinished building on a concrete floor. My children managed to get here with help from neighbors. My husband is again with me. He's a cripple now. He'll never walk again. Life is hard here. The people are very hostile sometimes. But we'll stay here until our village is safe to return to. The time has not yet come. People are still being murdered there. Last night in Gulak, Boko Haram stabbed nine men to death. My uncle was one of them. They took his two wives and his two daughters with them. My uncle's family had actually fled to Yola. They were living with us. But a few days ago they decided to return to our village. These are the final days of the sowing season. If you don't plant now, you'll have nothing to harvest for the rest of the year.

I have become very strange. I cannot concentrate as well as before. I am afraid of open spaces, large squares, broad streets. And the nightmares. I often dream that Shekau is chasing me. That's what Boko Haram says: You can never hide from Shekau. Shekau will always get you.

"To you my dear brethren, Muslims, those who are true believers and not those who practice democracy, not those who believe in the constitution, not those who believe in Western education. My regards to my leaders like Mullar Umar, the Amirul Muminin in Afghanistan; great minds like Sheikh Al Zawahiri; those like the Amir of Yemen, Abu Basir; the likes of Abu Mus'ab Abdul Wudud; and others in Pakistan and Iran, like Al-Baghadad. My greetings go to you all. I thank you all."

—*Abubakar Shekau, July 2014*

# IN THE HOUSE OF SULE HELAMU

We are sitting on wooden benches across from one another. Naked earth is beneath our feet. The sixteen-year-old Clara has wrapped herself in a thin, white cloth. She leans forward and kneads her toes with her fingers. Her voice is a whisper. This interview takes place over two days. She will show us her face only on the second day. Just a bit after our conversation had started we wanted to stop because we had the impression our questions were too painful for Clara, but she insisted she wanted to continue. She wanted to tell her story.

She is a Christian, and for this reason we found ourselves at the Catholic parish of St. Theresa in Yola. This is the seat of the bishop. We asked a priest to find us a quiet place where we could talk, but he found this difficult. There are people all over the church grounds. The place of contemplation has become a place where refugees come to find sanctuary. Almost all are Christians who have been expelled from their villages in the North. Now, in July 2015, there are considerably fewer than there were four months before. The fighting has tapered off. Many people have found the courage—or become desperate enough—to return to their villages. Nevertheless, the large expanse of the church lands is still overcrowded.

We sit behind one of the dormitories, close to the damp, gray wall that surrounds the premises. This is one of the few places where one is left alone. But this is also the place where innumerable blackflies get caught in our hair. Refugees use this area as a toilet at night. The priest apologizes for the smell but explains he could offer us no other place. We hear women gathered in choirs singing in front of the statues of saints stationed around the vast yard. Sometimes only one choir sings. At others, they all sing and drown each other out. They ask God for forgiveness, for strength, and for salvation from their suffering.

**Clara:** I really like to sing. In our parish, I sang in two choirs. After returning home, I'd be happy the rest of the day.

I come from a village near the city of Gulak. My father died when I was two. I don't remember him. He was supposed to have been a corn farmer. When I was four, my mother left us. She married again, and her new husband rejected us—my two sisters, my brother, and me. He did not want to take care of someone else's children. This is a tradition with us. I do not like this tradition. Since then, I have had no contact with my mother, even though she lives a few villages away. On foot, it takes only two hours to reach her. In all these years not once did I make the trip.

My mother rejected me. I struggle with myself. Everyone says I should not visit my mother. Her new husband wouldn't allow it anyway. I don't want my mother to have trouble because of me. I have often stood at the place where the path forks and have almost walked in the direction of my mother's village. She doesn't want me. But still I love my mother! I feel this. We cannot buy our parents at the market. Our parents will always be our parents.

She laughs for the first time, still playing with her toes.

**Clara:** My mother left me with an aunt. She passed her children off to different relatives. Up to that point, I'd seen my aunt only at funerals. Her name is Rhoda. I lived in her house for thirteen years. I suffered a lot. My aunt had given birth to ten children. Four of them died shortly after birth. She is an evil woman. She treated me like a slave. She hit me often. She hit me when it was time to wake up at five in the morning. She hit me with a thin stick. She woke her own children at the same time but did not hit them. The first thing I did in the morning was fetch water. I took a big bucket on my head and went to the well five or six times. Then I washed the dishes from the previous day, and then I washed the aunt's little children. They didn't want to be washed and would often run away. Sometimes they threw stones at me. "You are living in our father's house!" they would say. I washed all the children who were younger than five. I put fresh clothes on them. They would make themselves dirty with sand on purpose so that they could tell their mother I hadn't washed them.

Clara lived with Rhoda's children in a one-story mud house with seven rooms. There was a storeroom with peanuts, corn, and millet in gunnysacks. Rats flitted between the sacks. Clara was scared of the rats. At some point they became a real nuisance because Rhoda couldn't afford pesticide. To the left of the storeroom was the kitchen, with two fireplaces, two large iron pots, and four smaller ones. One room farther along was Rhoda's room. Clara remembers it as the most comfortable room in the house. It had one window and was cool even in summer. The house had no furnishings, only sacks in which the family kept its clothes. Behind Rhoda's room was the room for the older girls. Clara slept here.

**Clara:** I could finally wash myself an hour after waking up in the morning. I had to work so much in the home that I was often late to school. We were punished at school for being late. The teacher would hit you on the bottom. Most teachers did not hit us hard so that it hurt, but some really enjoyed it. At break, I'd have to run home fast because I had to cook for the family. For twenty people. Millet porridge. After that, I ran back to school. There were thirty-five students in my class. I was in the ninth grade. I love school. I love to read so much.

My best friend's name is Zainab. She is Muslim and sits next to me. At first, we actually did not like each other at all. We had a big argument early on. Zainab is supposed to read from a book to the class, but she isn't able to so well, so the teacher hits her. I laugh at her with the other girls. Zainab is already eighteen. I say to her, "You always pretend to be such a big lady, and you can't even do that." Out on the school yard, she then jumps me and rips my uniform. We hit each other, fall to the ground, kick each other. Then the teacher comes, pulls us apart, and hits us both with a branch that he broke from a tree.

That evening I went to Zainab's house, which was near ours. "What do you want here?" she demanded. "You stupid cow!" I apologized to her and asked her to forgive me. I asked her to take a walk with me. To help me pick herbs for cooking. From then on, we were friends. We always wanted to be together. We lent each other clothes. Sometimes she'd wear my things, sometimes I'd wear hers. The uncle, Rhoda's husband, did not like that. He did not like it because Zainab was Muslim. My uncle likes to drink a lot. They distill schnapps from millet in the village. He is violent when he is drunk. He'd hit anyone in the house. He even hit Aunt Rhoda when she was pregnant with the twins three years ago. God will make him pay for all the things he did to us. I am sure of that.

My uncle treats the village's sick animals. That's how he supported us. He looked after cows, goats, and sheep. He works in the morning and drinks at night. He'd often stumble into my room at night and tell me I had to go back to my mother now. By the next day, he'd already forgotten what he'd said. Often he'd throw me out of the house in the middle of the night. He called my mother a whore and me a bastard. "You must have patience," said Zainab to me after nights like that. "Be strong. Someday this will be over."

A year ago was when I heard of Boko Haram for the first time. We were to sing at church, to give courage to the Christians so that they would hold on to their faith. It was a Saturday. We were practicing a song for Sunday mass. "When Will You Come Back, Oh Jesus?" We sang for two hours. The choir leader was called

Mommy and she was nice. The next day I saw her dead on the street.

The chances of ending the bloodletting through negotiation were never good. Since Boko Haram's founding, there have been a few attempts. Representatives of both sides had frequently met secretly, but these advances always failed. The first attempt at rapprochement was in spring 2012, but the negotiations were suddenly suspended because a Boko Haram envoy was arrested during preparations for the talks. The second opportunity fell through because details of the negotiations were leaked in the press. Boko Haram accused the government of having sabotaged the talks. For the third attempt in June 2012, Shekau agreed to participate by telephone, but the *shura*, Boko Haram's supreme council, refused. The most promising attempt was the fourth one in May 2013, when Shekau sent a delegation of ten men to the Ivory Coast, where they are said to have come to an agreement with representatives of the Nigerian government. Reportedly, Shekau had already chosen a commander who was to go to Abuja and speak to selected members of the press to announce a cease-fire. This plan collapsed, however, as in June the U.S. government declared it would pay 7 million dollars for Shekau's capture. Then, in July, a new video from Shekau appeared. He refused to participate in any further negotiations and called on his followers to raid schools.

Both sides in this conflict are internally divided. On the government side, many politicians and members of the military find negotiating with terrorists shameful. Others openly thwart any advances toward dialogue because a cease-fire would endanger their local business and political interests. War allows corruption to bloom, and many army officers earn their best money this way. Police squads and military units earn more money during war than at peacetime. They collect bribe money at roadblocks, money they would not have if they were back in their barracks. On the

other side, it is unclear who speaks for Boko Haram. Men who
in the past claimed to represent the group were often exposed as
frauds. No one knows how much influence Shekau really has, or
if he is in fact dead and kept, as a symbol of Boko Haram's invin-
cibility, artificially alive through multiple doubles. Has "Shekau,"
perhaps, already become a kind of honorary title?

**Clara:** They came in the evening. We always went to bed at eight
o'clock. Our dog barked and woke us up. Outside, I heard the
sound of tank treads. First I thought soldiers were coming, since
they used tanks. Then we heard cries of "Allahu Akbar!" They
ran from all sides into the village. They arrived at our house and
banged on the door with the butts of their guns. Our dog kept
barking. So they shot at the dog. My aunt had named him Rambo.
I loved that dog very much. I fed him every day. His fur was red
and white, but his nose was all white.

We interrupt the interview because all at once the choirs around
the church compound have gone quiet. We hear agitated shouts.
Clara frowns. Only two kilometers away a bomb has exploded.
Clara's telephone rings. A friend asks her if she is all right, whether she knows anything about the bomb. She says she doesn't
know. Suddenly, a lot of telephones are ringing. Here and there we
see women running in different directions. Is somebody attacking the church? The priests here have long feared this might happen. The church employs guards around its property, but they are
unarmed, and they are wispy old men who would not be able to
keep anyone at bay for long. For Sunday mass, the police arrive
with security forces and scanners. Today, however, is Saturday.

Finally, a priest is able to reach a police officer at a nearby station. He gives the all-clear. Apparently, a nine-year-old boy had
been carrying a large metal object, a block that was much too
heavy for him. He was hauling it in the direction of the police
station. A scrap metal dealer, one of the many lining Yola's main

street fishing for customers, went over to him. He wanted the metal. The dealer saw that he was in fact carrying a bomb and yelled at the boy. The child threw the metal object away from himself, but not far enough. The explosion lacerated his leg. He later told the police that strangers gave him money to take the bomb and leave it somewhere close to the police station. The detective assumed this was a Boko Haram bomb. The boy was treated by a doctor and disappeared into one of the police station's interrogation rooms. No one knows what's going to happen to him there or how long he will be held.

Clara is now too nervous to carry on the conversation. We are too; we quickly call our driver. At this point, we still can't be sure the attempted attack was not meant for us. We take leave of one another and agree to meet the next day.

That night, Yola is quiet. The next morning, we drive to the parish center and return with Clara to the same place by the wall and sit on the same benches.

**Clara:** The men kept beating the doors with their guns. The whole house was filled with noise. They had shot at our dog Rambo but not hit him. I was so afraid I peed in my dress. Aunt Rhoda shat her dress. But we were lucky. The military returned then. The soldiers and the Boko Haram fighters spent many hours shooting at one another. As Boko Haram retreated, they blew up the village clinic. I saw the ruins when we finally escaped. I also saw our pastor, the one who had baptized me, lying dead in front of his door. They had shot him in the belly.

Almost everyone in the village fled. Boko Haram attacked it again and again. My aunt and her children went to Yola. The uncle stayed in the house. He said, "No one is going to force me to leave my own home." I was sent to my grandma in Gulak. My friend Zainab also came with me. Her mother told her to go with me to Gulak. She slept the night there, and the next day I took her to the bus stop so she could go to her grandmother in Yola. We cried and hugged one another. "Clara," she said as we left each other, "may God have mercy on all of us." Since then I have had no news of her—not until yesterday.

She is supposed to be living with her mother in Yola now. They say her mother married a Boko Haram fighter of her own free will. One of them! I can hardly believe it! Before, she had nothing to do with them. Her first husband, the father of Zainab, was in the village militia. He was not a good man. He hit her a lot. Just before the attack he hit her so hard that she had a miscarriage. He always hit her in the belly.

In Gulak, I saw my grandma for the first time. She did not have the money to send me to school. Gulak is a bigger city. The school fees are not six hundred naira a month, as they are in our village, but a thousand (*about five euros*). Grandma told me to earn the money to pay them myself. I tried to find work on the fields, but that's not easy. The farmers say girls my age are too small and lazy. They want older girls.

Gulak is a young city, like Gubla and Duhu. To the east rise the Mandara Mountains, where the animists of Sukur live. At just one thousand meters, these giant granite cones are not especially high, but they are very rugged and inaccessible. To the west is a wide plain that gradually turns into the Sambisa Forest. Gulak is on the A13. British Protestant missionaries, who built a school and a clinic at the foot of the mountains, founded Gulak. Today, it has five thousand residents, equal parts Christian and Muslim, and it is the seat of a district administration. It is the center of a little cosmos of thirty villages together.

When the A13 was built in the 1980s, it served as a gateway to modernity, bringing ideas, goods, and new people to the region. Boko Haram now uses this highway as its axis of aggression. Starting from the Sambisa, it took over village after village. In Gulak, once again three thousand military personnel gathered to repel Boko Haram and to initiate a counteroffensive. The city administration tried to assure the residents that the city could not be taken. Radio channels praised the strength of the army. Most residents trusted that the military would succeed. The schools were left open to the end. People thought they were safe. They stayed in Gulak until the avoidable became unavoidable.

**Clara:** I lived for two months in Gulak. Then Boko Haram came here, too. "Run!" cried the soldiers, who were also racing away in their jeeps and tanks. "Run!"

It was five in the evening. We heard shots in the distance. Grandma froze. She stood in front of her house and did not move. I said, "Grandma, we need to get in the house!" I pulled at her. I said, "Grandma, we will be shot if we stay here!" But she just stood there. I started to cry, and then I ran away. I ran in the same direction everyone else ran—to the main road and then into the bush. I don't know how long I ran, but suddenly I saw Aunt Rhoda. This whole time she'd hidden up in the mountains in a small village, and now she, too, was on the run. I cried. She cried. We hugged. She had always treated me like a slave, but now there was no slave, no master. Four of her children went missing during her escape. She didn't know where they were. Only the twins were with her. One she carried on her back, the other she cradled in one arm.

I took one of the twins from her, but all at once, as we were crossing an open area of scrubland, I didn't see Rhoda anymore. I saw so many people running across the scrubland. But no Rhoda! The child in my arms cried. It wanted breast milk. It was only nine months old. And I myself had nothing to drink. I was so thirsty. I kept running. We spent the night in a grain field. I covered the baby with my wrap to keep the mosquitos off it.

The next morning I reached a village where I asked after my aunt. But no one knew anything. Later, I met a group of women in this village who were also fleeing south, and I joined them. They helped me with the baby when we crossed rivers. I'd not have been able to carry the baby to the other shore alone. The little one's name is Hussaina.

For the next six days, I was alone with the baby. Sometimes I slept in the bush, sometimes in a small village. On the seventh day, I finally found Rhoda. She had waited for me in a village along the national road and hoped that I or one of her four children would stop there. Rhoda looked tired. Her clothes were ripped. I never liked her, but now I felt sorry for her. I gave the baby back to Rhoda. He'd gotten used to me by that point and did not want to return to his mother. When Rhoda took him and hugged him, Hussaina wriggled around and screamed for me. He wanted to come back to me.

She grins.

Then together we looked for the other four children—four girls. They were between four and nine years old. Small children often stay behind when people run away. They are like pebbles washed up onto the banks of a river. You see them on the edges of the big streets. We searched from village to village. We even turned and went in the direction of Boko Haram. We heard shots in the distance, and that's when we finally found them. The priest of a small village had taken in twenty children. All of them had lost their parents. He let them sleep at his house at night. During the day, he took them to the main road so that their parents might see them as they fled to the south.

I thanked God in my prayers. He had saved us. But one day later disaster struck. Boko Haram fighters were suddenly everywhere. They had come on the main road from the north and swept through several villages along the main road. Aunt Rhoda had just sent me to a seamstress. On the way there, suddenly I saw the fighters in front of me and behind me.

———

Every day of this conflict made Boko Haram stronger. As long as the group is on the move it can fill its arsenals with plunder. War feeds more war. The fighters who previously had only Kalashnikovs and homemade explosives at their disposal now have tanks. In many places around Nigeria, Boko Haram fought the military with superior firepower. They are equipped with dozens of armored personnel carriers and heavy battle tanks, mortars, and air defense guns. In summer 2014, they shot a Nigerian air force jet out of the sky and beheaded one of the two pilots in front of a rolling camera.

Boko Haram also capture weaponry and buy it. They buy most of it on Nigeria's black market, as the Nigerian army does. West Africa is a subcontinent of porous borders and smugglers' routes. There are reportedly ten thousand unsecured border crossings connecting Niger, Chad, Nigeria, and Cameroon. Weaponry from Muammar Gaddafi's giant depots at first landed in Mali but then ended up in Nigeria with Boko Haram. There are indications that Boko Haram emissaries use their Kanuri contacts to buy weaponry directly from south Libya. Weapons are smuggled from Cameroon, Niger, and Chad. The sect obtains most ordnance in Nigeria itself, for if there is one thing not in short supply in this conflict-ridden land it is weapons.

**Clara:** I ran up a hill with a group of girls. We fled from the village as Boko Haram stormed it. My aunt and the children were all still there. We ran, and suddenly we heard gunshots right in front of us. So we ran in the opposite direction, down the hill. That was a mistake. We didn't realize we were running from an echo, so Boko Haram was behind us! We ran straight into their arms! I fled through tall grass, jumped over low bushes. I lost my sandals and stepped onto many thorns. Then I saw the first of them: a big man with a beard. He wore a uniform. I ran past him. He smiled. A little while later there was another one, with a black turban. He called, "Stop!" I tried to run past him, but he shot into the air. I fell in terror and rolled down a slope. Then, I saw five men coming. They bent down over me, and I became dizzy, and then I passed out.

When I awoke, I was with some other girls on a flatbed pulled by a trike. The back of my head kept smacking hard against the metal surface. The men had tied my arms behind my back with rags. They had covered my eyes, but I managed to move the blindfold a bit so I could see where they took us.

They drove us back to Gulak and took us to a big house that had earlier belonged to Sule Helamu. He was rich and had worked for the city administration. A high wall topped with barbed wire surrounded the house. A big neem tree grew in front of it. The house's roof was the color of ox blood. They untied us once we were in the inner courtyard. They pulled me by the arms from the flatbed. I saw in front of me a man with a wild beard. He lifted his arms. "God is great! We have new guests!" he said. Then he looked right at me and said, "From now on we will call you Fatima." He gave me a long veil and told me to wear it from then on. Many women were already crouching in the courtyard. It was really crowded because there were so many women there. They were preparing their food and hardly looked at us. We were led by the men through the crowd.

I think there were more than one hundred women and about two hundred children. They slept in two rooms but at least during the day were allowed to be in the sun. The younger women were kept in a building built against the courtyard wall. They took us there and opened the door to a room. I looked in and saw only darkness. I screamed, "I won't go in!" I threw myself on the ground. They kicked me, pulled me, and tried to drag me in. They screamed, "You cockroach! You worm!" I begged back, "Let me go to my grandma!" Then, from inside the room I heard a girl's voice that said in the language of my village, "Come to us. Those men will kill you otherwise."

The room was as big as a small hut in our village. There was no toilet, just a hole in the ground. When we'd done our business, we'd rinse our shit down the hole. A lot of the time we had no water. Then we just did it in the corner. Pretty soon the corner was full of shit. They gave us water every few days so we could at least clean a little.

At four in the morning, they'd open the door for a few minutes for morning prayer. Then, they locked it again until evening, when they would again open it for a while. It was almost completely dark in the room, even during the day. But they gave us a flashlight. When the batteries died, they gave us new ones.

After a week, the door opened at an unusual time. They called us out. It was around midday. They told us to stand in a row. There were two captured men in the courtyard; one was lying down, the other kneeled. They wore government uniforms. The emir gave a short speech. He told us that these men had been guards at the federal prison. The one lying down begged for water. He had blood between his fingers. "This man," said the emir, "has violated the will of God. We will kill anyone, even our own fathers, who acts against God's will."

Boko Haram had hoisted its own black flag over the building. They dragged one of the men so that he was in front of us so we could all see him. His hands were tied to a stick. They had tied his hands fast to the stick. He could barely move. I wanted to look away, but the Boko Haram men shouted at me. "Look!" they said. "Look at him!" One held the man's head between two hands and forced him to lean forward. Another began to cut from behind, through the neck muscle. The first of the captives was a tall, fat man. He screamed, "Oh God! Receive me into your kingdom!" It took twenty minutes. That's how long the executioner took to cut through his neck. That's how long this man hung between life and death. Then the fighters shot their guns into the air.

When they turned to the second man who was lying on the ground, he did not move. They shook him and saw he was already dead. I do not know what he died of.

The next day I was sick and had a fever. I couldn't walk. The Boko Haram men brought a doctor who gave me two intravenous drips.

I lived in that house for five months, from September 2014 to January 2015. We had to pray all day, and when we didn't pray we had lessons in Islam. The older women in the courtyard had warned us, "As soon as you know the Koran well enough, the men will marry you off." I tricked them and made mistakes on purpose while reciting. I cannot betray Jesus.

Our teacher was named Abu Yusuf. He once hit me with a fan belt so hard that I thought he would kill me. He ripped open the skin on my legs and I bled. They are still full of scars. I had not recited a passage of the Koran well enough for him. Abu Yusuf's emir took him to task. We always called this emir "Kaka," or "grandfather." "Why are you hitting the girl so hard," he asked. "We are here to realize God's will, but you are hitting her too hard."

Yusuf was small and very young. He had no beard, but had long hair with wild ringlets. He was so young, but he always looked so serious. He often wore military clothes and a bulletproof vest. I think he was a Kanuri. The younger Boko Haram fighters were often more cruel than the older ones. Abu Yusuf carried a whip over his shoulder. Every day he came to the courtyard on a bike. There were always two whips hanging off the handlebars. That's why we were so afraid of him.

In the room where they had squeezed us in were twenty-one girls, but mostly I was with the three girls with whom I had been captured on the hill. We had our own corner. Their names were Janet, Hadja, and Hassana. The fighters renamed Hassana Mariam. She was very quiet but very smart. She said to me that when we knelt down to pray we secretly make a Christian prayer.

The fighters gave us dates with water to drink, but we did not drink it. We were suspicious. Maybe they had bewitched the water. I remember how in the courtyard the fighters stood in a long row, a man pouring a potion from a calabash gourd into a small cup. They did this once or twice a week. They told us one day to make tea, and they brought us a bucket with red water and said we should tip it in the tea before we drink it. We did not do this. You have to watch out for Boko Haram. They have many tricks.

One day, they celebrated in the courtyard. They set up a radio, a black box with a long antenna. They turned it up loud and listened to the news. When they heard the reporter say that a woman had blown herself up in a mosque in the city of Kano, they cheered. They danced with joy. The assassin was one of their wives. She was the wife of Mohammed. Her name was Aisha. She killed many dozens of people in Kano. Mohammed had three children with Aisha, and after her death his other two wives took the children. Mohammed was a nice man. He sometimes brought us food. Sometimes he was with us. And then he was gone for weeks, fighting somewhere. The wives of Mohammed were presented to us as model women. One was even younger than I. These women were very mean to us. If we did not wear our head scarves, they would scold us loudly. But they never hit us. They wore black niqabs. Their faces were almost entirely covered. I saw only their eyes.

A little bit after the radio report, one of the Boko Haram commanders came to us. His name was Wal Arab, the "son of the Arab." He gave a little speech. He said we would be divided into different groups. One group would be married off, the other trained for suicide bombings. Wal Arab said that they had begun suicide attacks using their own Kanuri wives, and that now they would offer us, the Margi women, the honor of sacrificing ourselves to God. "When you die, you will go to paradise." We began to cry. "Do not weep," he said. "Many of us have already lost our own wives. Some of us have lost our entire families."

———

In its open war against the military, Shekau's sect broke a further taboo. Only a few weeks after abducting the Chibok girls in June 2014, Boko Haram turned kidnapped girls into weapons for the first time. The group had succeeded in converting a few of them into compliant followers of their madness. Most of the girls, however, were forced into it. One woman in her early twenties initiated the suicide attacks in the city of Gombe. She rode a motorcycle with a bomb to the entrance of a military base. She killed herself and a soldier. By January 2016, 120 girls, some only nine years old, had carried out suicide attacks. They killed 750 people and injured 1,200. Most of the girls had been kidnapped just months before the attacks. Inconspicuous, they are rarely noticed at checkpoints, and they wear flowing hijabs, garments that allow explosives to be transported undetected.

The girls kill themselves in buses full of passengers, at marketplaces where thousands push and shove. They attack at checkpoints and administrative facilities. Boko Haram sends out suicide bombers in waves. On December 30, 2015, fourteen of them made their way to Maiduguri, but twelve were stopped and detained. Only two managed to set off their explosives. According to the Nigerian police, two men usually accompany the bomb transporters. Many of the younger girls have no idea what they are carrying. One man watches from a distance to make sure the girl is moving in the right direction. This is also the one who sets off the bomb with a call from a mobile telephone. Another man follows her to ensure she does not run away.

The Tamil Tigers in Sri Lanka, members of the PKK (Kurdistan Workers' Party), and the extremists in Chechnya all use suicide bombers. However, they all turn to them in times of weakness. But Shekau's men began using suicide attacks at the height of their success. No Boko Haram weapon has killed more people than the kidnapped girls. In Yola alone in December 2015, more than one hundred people were killed by suicide attacks. These days women are changing their fashions because they are afraid of being shot by nervous soldiers. They shorten their dresses or wear a hijab in combination with light shirts.

Clara and her fellow hostages were lucky. A few of them were trained to use rifles. None, however, were chosen to be suicide bombers.

**Clara:** Every two weeks, most of the men would leave the grounds. The older women told us they were going to the front. A few days later, they'd be back with pickup trucks full of stolen goods, stuff they'd plundered along the way. TVs and refrigerators and computers. Sometimes they brought back hostages. They'd kill them in our courtyard. I think they wanted to make us afraid so that we'd obey them even more. They shot some and beheaded others. Some they killed because they refused to join the religion of the true God. Others they killed because they did not want to fight with Boko Haram.

Almost every day they brought new girls to the house. They cried. Many panicked. I also saw some who at first were stiff, numb. They did not speak. They just sat there. In our dungeon, we said, "Calm down. Don't give up. They are giving us food. They are keeping us alive." This is what the others girls had told us the first day when we arrived.

The smallest girl was two years old. Her name was Precious, and she cried a lot. She cowered the whole time next to me. The fighters told me I must take care of her. She was sick and threw up a lot. Her barf was everywhere—on the floor, under me, even on me, on my clothes. At some point, I told the fighters I could not take care of her anymore. The teacher Abu Yusuf gave the baby to one of the fighter's wives. She lived away from the camp. When he took her, he said, "What kind of a person are you? Would you just reject your own child this way?" And I answered back, "What sort of people are you? You stole that baby from her parents."

After three months, they brought us before the emir. We stood in his office, and he looked at us. It was the beginning of

December. He said our time had come. We would all be married in the next two weeks. When some of us started to cry, he said, "Are you better than the Chibok girls? By now, they understand our religion. They would even cut the throats of their parents!" The emir then read out the names of our husbands. I was to marry Wal Arab. He stood to the left of the emir and smiled. I do not know why he smiled. Wal Arab always cooked in the courtyard for the fighters. He had never spoken a word to me. Now he asked me, "Do you love me?" I did not answer him. I remained silent. It was on this day I decided I definitely had to escape.

One after the other we were married off. One after the other we were taken from our room. After a while, they even married a ten-year-old girl to a fighter. I do not remember her real name. I only remember that they renamed her Ummi. She was as tall as I but had no breasts. They trapped this girl and told her that they were taking her back to her parents. Ummi did not know she was to be married. She was allowed to visit us one time after that, after about a month. She told me she was married to the man who had captured me on the hill. She stayed a whole day with us, but after that, we never saw her again.

She said she would lock herself in her room a lot, she told me on her last visit. She had to wear a burka, even though she was still so small, because she was now a real wife. Her husband shouted at her often because she could not cook well, but she said he never hit her. "If I have the chance, I am going to run away," she said.

They postponed my wedding many times because I hadn't learned the Koran. Five girls were married before me. One said to me before she left, "I am afraid that the man has HIV." She was married to one of the emir's deputies and was his fourth wife. A second said to me, "Tell my mother I love her very much." Early in the morning she was taken outside and driven away on the backseat of a motorcycle. A third and a fourth girl were Muslims and married to the same man, the one who brought the firewood. I have heard nothing from any of these women.

It was not easy to plan our escape. We wanted to flee together, my three friends and I. We could trust no one else. Many of the other girls had changed over the months. They had accepted their fate and were "ready," as the fighters said. At first, they resisted their situation. Now, they were the first to run outside for Koran lessons. We did not trust them anymore. We whispered together in our corner of the room, my three friends and I. When the others asked what we were whispering about, we'd say, "Nothing important."

Before us, four other girls had tried to escape. Two made it through the gate but were captured a few meters outside. The other two made it over the wall with a ladder but jumped down on the other side right in front of a Boko Haram man. They were flogged, taken back to our room, and not allowed outside for many days.

At one point, I had diarrhea and called through the door that they must let me outside to go to a proper toilet. But they did not open the door. So I squatted over a tin plate. I put the plate right at the door. When the guard came through the door that morning, he stepped in my shit. He hit me hard, but from then on they left the door open. That was important for our plan.

We waited. Then one day most of the men had left the house of Sule Helamu to go to the southern front to fight. Six remained behind: five in a room, talking, and only one who guarded us. It was late morning. I told him I wanted to fetch spices for cooking. They kept the spices at the other end of the courtyard. The fighters had brought back a goat head that they wanted us to prepare. I asked for pepper. We took blankets, to rappel down the wall, and niqabs. We were very afraid. We climbed up a ladder. Once at the top of the wall, I threw a blanket over the barbed wire. Even so, we hurt ourselves because the barbs pushed through the blanket. That hurt a lot. Janet injured her foot and could only hobble along. Just behind the wall grew a tree. We reached out and held on to its branches and then jumped. We were lucky. No one had seen us!

We put on our niqabs and went along the main road. My feet trembled. We looked like the wives of Boko Haram men. Suddenly, four of the fighters drove up to us on motorcycles. They blocked our way and asked, "Who are you?" We answered that we are the wives of the *rijale*. That is what Boko Haram men call themselves. *Rijale* means "the strong men." They told us to show our faces. We answered that our husbands would not allow that. I knew the men who had stopped us. They guarded our house from time to time. If we had shown our faces, they would have recognized us.

When we reached the edge of Gulak and saw the fields of millet before us, we ran. In the fields, we took off our niqabs and threw them into the bushes and kept on running. After a night, we came to the village of Pallam, where we met an old woman. She warned us that other escaped women had found our niqabs and put them on. The fighters captured them, believing they were us. "They are looking for you! Run!" said the woman. So we ran back into the bush, away from villages and streets.

On the evening of the second day, we were getting close to Cameroon. We met no people. There was no one but us. We walked past burned-down houses and destroyed churches. At some point, we met a man riding a donkey. We followed him for a while until his path led elsewhere. He pointed and showed us the way to Cameroon. We were hungry. I was sick and still had diarrhea. Our feet were badly swollen. Janet could barely walk.

When we reached the border, we saw the corpses of two women and a man. The man was half naked. His shirt hung in rags from the branches of a tree. They were all in a ditch next to the street and stank. We later learned that Cameroonian soldiers had shot them because they thought they were Boko Haram. That's when we realized we'd gone from one dangerous situation to another one.

The war in Nigeria has also impinged upon Cameroon since 2014. For Boko Haram, the border between the two countries doesn't exist. The group used northern Cameroon as a place where its troops can recuperate. Boko Haram has also recruited hundreds of new members from this region, and it operates training camps here where children kidnapped in Nigeria are prepared for war. It is said they are only between ten and fourteen years of age. Currently, five thousand child soldiers are under the command of Boko Haram.

As in Nigeria, the north of Cameroon is economically dependent on the south. The people live in squalor and hardship. Poverty is increasing. The payment that Boko Haram offers its fighters is very attractive. Also, as in Nigeria, state institutions inspire little confidence. Corruption has undermined state structures. Cameroon's president, who has been in power since 1982, is eighty-two years old. It is not at all clear who will succeed him, and a power struggle threatens state stability. Kanuri, the tribe that supplies Boko Haram with most of its members, live on both sides of the border.

Boko Haram compensates for its losses in Nigeria with victories in Cameroon and vice versa. It occupied several cities just over the border, with hundreds of people dying between the fronts. Anyone who did not flee right away after the seizure of his or her village in Cameroon was suspected by Cameroonian security forces of belonging to Boko Haram. Cameroon's army is also known for its brutality. In December 2015, in an act of retaliation, it attacked the city of Gwoza, the former Boko Haram headquarters, and killed more than seventy civilians.

**Clara:** In the first village after the border we met a group of young men. "Where do you come from?" they asked us. We said we were coming home from working in the fields. They did not believe us. They threatened us and said we had to give them money or they would tell soldiers we didn't belong there. They got more and more aggressive and pulled on our arms. But then a miracle happened.

One of the village women helped us. She said to the young men, "These girls have been living here a long time." They let us go but still demanded money: three hundred naira. The woman gave them the money. She was Muslim. This night we slept at her house. She also came from Gulak. She gave us water and something to eat: tuwo and karkashi soup with dumplings. It was delicious.

Janet was the youngest, fourteen, and she couldn't go on. She was a Christian from Gulak. Boko Haram kidnapped her from her parents' house. We left her with the woman. She promised to put Janet on the bus to Yola in one or two days, when she was stronger. Since we left her in Cameroon, we have heard nothing from her.

I now live in Yola with my older sister and her husband. I'd like to go back to school, but I have no money for the uniform and books. So they won't let me go back to school. I often think of my mother. I've heard she is ready to meet with me. That is what I want most. I will meet my mother in her village once the roads are safer again. I think my mother loves me. I believe this.

"Free yourself from great fear. Let yourself be freed from hellfire. Like you, seventy members of your family will marry seventy-two virgins in paradise. A crown of respect that will impress the prophet himself will be bestowed upon you. Keep your soul among the green birds of paradise. Check your desire to return to this world. Die as he died. Die for the blessings and rewards that will be yours after carrying out such a noble deed. I pray for you that you will be able to execute this precious act."

—*Audio file on a suicide bomber's cell phone, 2012*

# THE BONE

The rainy season, which brings with it the good and the bad, is a few weeks late this year. The sky over Yola is gray, the clouds gliding from the south and over the city. The sky is heavy every day, but still no rain. People look up more often than usual, in anticipation. This is the first rainy season after the catastrophe. Boko Haram destroyed most of the bridges. The rain, when it comes, will flood the rivers and carve the land into islands. For the first few days of the rainy season, people still get by with makeshift bridges, but later those are washed over or away. The rain will isolate villages and cities from one another for months. Whoever has business away from home attends to it now.

No one knows whose side the rain will take in this conflict. The army receives almost no reinforcements because road connections have been washed away. Will Boko Haram use this advantage to begin its attacks again? Or will the flooding also halt Boko Haram's operations? No one knows how many people will get sick and die this rainy season because they are unable to reach a doctor or a clinic. For in war, most people are killed not by bullets and grenades but by sickness and hunger.

Soundless lightning crazes the sky in the evenings, but no rain falls. I watch it from the hotel terrace. A radiant light. The horizon encircling us is a wreath of fire. The hotel's few guests gather around the terrace pool and stare uneasily in all directions.

The sofa Lydia sits on in the hotel is too large and wide for her. The seventeen-year-old presses herself into a corner of it, a blanket covering her. The air-conditioning is on too high. There are several flat-screen TVs. Modern African art is on the walls.

Lydia feels uneasy in this fancy place. It belongs to a part of

Nigeria that few Nigerians know: the world of luxury and abundance. Lydia will refuse to eat the food from here because it is alien to her.

Lydia has two very different faces: one that is bright and one that is dark. She has lived a few months already in Yola and helps out at a Catholic refugee center. She is a dynamo there, assisting with the distribution of clothes and bringing the sick to a doctor. She is one of the most cheerful people there, laughing heartily and encouraging people with small gestures. She is from Michika, fifty kilometers south of Gulak and also on national road A13. Her father was a doctor who worked at a local hospital. He died when she was thirteen.

**Lydia:** My father had a spell cast upon him. That is what everyone in our family said. They say his older brother, my uncle, put a curse on him. They always argued about who owned our house. It actually belonged to both of them. Their mother had built it and left it to them both. My uncle's family lived on one side of the courtyard, and we on the other. My father and uncle had different fathers. They always argued. My uncle told my father to move into his father's house. My uncle's family cast evil glances at us. My mother suspected they wanted to curse us, and they felt the same way. It was a serious problem.

My father became very sick from this fighting and lost his strength a bit every day because of this fight. He died after a few weeks. My mother married again. He was a neighbor. We all moved out, my younger brother Lucky and I, too. Our mother sent me to her mother in Mubi because she couldn't take care of us anymore. For three years now I have been living with my grandma.

Mubi is the second biggest city of the state of Adamawa and is two hundred kilometers from Yola. It is on the western bank of the Yedseram River, which loses itself in the swamps of the

Sambisa. Mubi is an economic motor of the Northeast. Almost all of Nigeria's major banks have branches here. The city has 130,000 residents and is a central hub between Cameroon and Nigeria. Merchants in Mubi trade in salt and diamonds, and one of the biggest cattle markets in Nigeria is here. As part of the German colonial empire, this region had German troops until 1914. A few buildings from the German colonial era still stand. The city has almost covered the entire valley where it is situated and is now spreading up the surrounding hills. To the east and west, giant granite boulders, rounded and gray, hem in the city.

Mubi is Christian and Muslim. Boko Haram surprise attacked the city on October 29, 2014. They renamed the city Madinatul Islam, which means "City of Islam." The fall of Mubi to the extremists seemed to foreshadow the end of Nigeria itself. Never before had victory for Boko Haram seemed so close. With the takeover of Mubi, Boko Haram controlled more than 180,000 square kilometers, almost 20 percent of Nigeria.

**Lydia:** It was an overcast day. As usual, I was up at six. As usual, I had to help Grandma Mariam in her restaurant. The name of the restaurant is Jadin Kowa. In English that means "Good for All." I slept in one room with the four waitresses who worked at the restaurant. They always got up an hour earlier than I did in the morning and had left by the time I woke up. My grandma is a difficult woman: greedy and grumbly. She gave her waitresses little to eat. If they ate too much, she screamed at them. I liked the waitresses. They weren't smart, but they were my best friends.

That day I woke up and went with my brother Lucky, who is eleven, and my grandmother to the restaurant. On the way, everything was the same as always. Grandma and I talked about customers, about the ones who always buy on credit and never pay. She said we did not earn enough. She said the girls made the portions so big that we were not making a profit. She complained that they still hadn't learned to flavor the soups properly, though she was the one who refused to give them enough spices. Too little salt, too little Maggi. The girls and Grandma always argued, but never in front of the customers. "Go fuck your father!" she'd scream at them when she was sure the customers couldn't hear.

Grandma's restaurant was at the bus station. There are a lot of people and buses and trikes there. It is very loud. You hear the bus drivers honking their horns, the shouting of people, and music. The store owners put big loudspeakers on the street to attract customers. They usually play hip-hop. I love hip-hop. I listen to it almost the whole day. I usually have earbuds in both ears. But when I am in the restaurant, I put only one bud in an ear so I can hear the customers.

The restaurant has two tables inside and three outside. The girls cook and serve food, while Grandma works the cash register. She sits the whole day on a white plastic chair near the entrance. Coca-Cola ads hang on the walls. We serve pepper soup with three pieces of meat in it for 250 naira (*about one euro*). If it has only one piece of meat in it, the soup costs 150 naira. Even cheaper is the rice and bean porridge that costs only 100 naira.

When we arrived that morning, the girls had already swept the floor and cooked the food. The restaurant is open from seven in the morning to seven at night. I served drinks. My grandma has a small refrigerator, and I put some food in there, first thing. She went to the market to buy meat and spices. The city was still quiet. The customers talked this morning about the Boko Haram insurgents. Some said they would come, others said they would not. They only attacked the villages and small cities that the military did not protect. That's what my grandma always said, too. There were so many soldiers in Mubi. We thought we would be safe. Still, for days there were rumors that they would attack, and every time panic broke out. But people also seemed to have gotten used to it.

Then, after the lunch break, people in and around the bus station suddenly started running. Even our customers ran. They just left their meals where they were. They said Mubi was being boxed in from three sides. Only the south, in the direction of Yola, was open. We ran, too, the girls and I. Grandma was still at the market. We left our customers sitting where they were at their tables. Lucky had already run away. Just like that. As we dashed through the city we heard the first shots. We ran home, looking for my brother, calling into every room, searching everywhere. Grandma came in with her groceries from the market. "Where's Lucky? We have to find him!" she cried. "We've already looked everywhere!" I screamed. Then one of the waitresses said, "Be quiet! They are outside the house."

We were silent. I could hear my heart's beat. Then a quiet voice just outside spoke. "Open the door!" The voice was very soft. I unlocked the padlock and opened the door. So many Boko Haram men stood in front of our house. I don't know how many there were anymore. "Are there any men in the house?" the one with the soft voice asked. He was still very young. Handsome. Another one searched the house, and then we had to follow them out into the street. A man closed the door behind us. We went to the main road, where we saw corpses. They had simply tossed the bodies one on top of the other. They were in a heap. I saw the tiny arms and legs of children sticking out. More than twenty dead. The main road was splattered with blood.

They led us past a few houses and then took us into one of them and locked it. I knew the house. It belonged to the man who repaired our satellite dish. He'd already fled the city. The Boko Haram men said, "Become Islam, and we let you go. If not, we kill you." Grandma blurted out, "We will become Muslim!" We sat on the floor. We were bewildered. They brought us food and Coke. The others drank the Coke they brought, but I didn't. I thought about Lucky the whole time.

Outside the shooting was still going on. I didn't know at first why they were shooting. Days later one of the militants told me that they had taken all the men they could catch to the same spot.

This was the place in the street that we'd seen, the one with the corpses. That's where they shot them. "We kill them," a fighter said, "because they are infidels."

They left us alone for the night. Even more women were brought to the house. By the end, we were maybe about one hundred. Many were our neighbors. They looked very different now. They trembled, had red eyes and ripped clothes. If the fighters found a cell phone on anyone, they took it away it. I managed to hide mine and sent a text to my mother. But she didn't answer.

The next morning we heard only a few shots outside in the city. I had calmed down a little. Only a few women were still crying. The fighters allowed us to be in the inner courtyard of the house. We sat there until afternoon. That's when we heard the sound of a jet overhead. The fighters drove us back into the house. I prayed. I was very afraid. Women hugged each other. Then I heard a loud blast, and after that nothing. All around me it was very quiet.

I lay on the floor. I couldn't see anything. It was black all around me. I saw only darkness. After a while, it grew brighter. There was so much dust in the air. I saw people, their outlines, but couldn't speak with them. I wasn't able to speak for a long time, even though I tried. I lay on my stomach. The bomb was a direct hit. A huge hole was in the roof. One wall had caved in. All the windows had been blown out. When my hearing finally came back, I heard the crying of a young child.

I called out the names of the four girls, the waitresses, but no one answered. I tried to get to the door, but I couldn't walk. I could only crawl. I saw the dead among the rubble, covered in dust and stone. Then I noticed I was bleeding heavily from my arm. The bone was broken. The arm itself stuck out to the side. Just the skin held my arm together. If I let it hang by my side, I thought it would rip off. A fighter carried me outside. Both my legs were also broken, but they didn't hurt yet. I didn't even notice they were broken. Then I saw the child, the one whose crying I had heard. It was a little girl. The bomb had shattered her leg. Later, it had to be cut off.

In front of the house, fighters carried away some corpses. They urgently called out commands, in Kanuri, which I do not speak. I speak Kamwe because I belong to the Higgi tribe. The fighter who carried me put me down in front of the house, got a motorcycle taxi, the kind with three wheels, and drove me to the outskirts of the city, to a house very close to the barracks. They had already seized that part of the city. They brought all wounded women to this house. They washed my wounds, gave me painkillers. Then they tried to fix me. They stitched me up in six places: one on the belly, two on the arm, and three on the leg.

Many women just ran after the explosion, but a lot were captured again the next morning. One of the waitresses was also wounded. She was in the house with me. She also had a broken leg. But Grandma and the other three had managed to escape. It is not kind of me to say this, but I was glad that not all of them had run away. I was relieved to have one of my friends with me.

Eventually, a Boko Haram woman came and looked after us. Her name was Miriam. I think she was twenty-three. Miriam wore a black burka and was alone with us. The fighters left only one man to guard the house. The others came and went. I stayed four weeks in this house. After two days, Boko Haram followers who understood something of medicine visited us. They splinted my arm. They splinted my legs.

Miriam told us she had been a Christian and married to a soldier in the Nigerian army. The Boko Haram militants killed him and kidnapped her. She said she was forced to marry the fighter who had killed her husband. But she quickly realized that this new husband earned more money than the old one. Things were much better with Boko Haram than they were with her former husband, she said. She told us we should follow her example.

Miriam gave me a new Muslim name. She called me Zainab. She was already pregnant with a child from her new husband. She was very strict. She hit girls with a cable when they didn't pay attention in Koran class. But she never hit me. I am a good student. I also tried hard to learn the Koran. I also find it easy to learn things by heart.

Miriam had a small, kidnapped boy at her side. Boko Haram gave him to her as a slave. She threatened to cut off our heads if we did not learn passages from the Koran well enough. She said that when our wounds healed Boko Haram would attach bombs to us and send us off as suicide bombers to the airport in Yola. Others of us would be married off.

I did not have my cell phone anymore. I lost it in the house that had been bombed. Also, Boko Haram had destroyed all the mobile phone antennae in the city. After two weeks, I still walked with great difficulty. There were now fourteen girls and four married women. The married women prayed a lot and fasted for our salvation. A few fighters visited to lead us in prayer. Every once in a while, fighters would show up looking for girls whose wounds had healed.

I wanted my legs to heal. They still hurt so much. I cried a lot. But then again, I did not want my legs to get better. I did not want a man to come and take me to the Sambisa.

But then the army returned to Mubi. It was November 23. Most of the Boko Haram fighters had to leave the city. They left Miriam behind. One early morning, when all the other girls were asleep, Miriam came to me and whispered that Boko Haram would soon abandon the city and the army would return. She asked me not to betray her.

"If I do this for you, what will you do for me?" I asked. "I will take you to your parents when you can walk again," she whispered. Miriam said she was happy the fighters would soon be gone. She also claimed she had always tried to stop Boko Haram from doing even worse things to us. So I promised not to betray her. Miriam became a different person after that. She cooked for us. She was friendly. She pleaded with us again and again to protect her.

After two days, Miriam packed away all the copies of the Koran and all the religious writings. The slave boy helped her. She turned to us and said she'd bring all the books back to the remaining Boko Haram commanders in the barracks. As soon as she went out, I heard shots.

Miriam came running back with the slave boy and the bag full of Korans because the military was just outside the barracks. The slave boy whispered to us, "The soldiers are here."

Miriam did not tell us this. She lied, "What you hear, those are the shots of the Boko Haram leaders. They are practicing so they can fight the army when it comes."

The next morning the soldiers were in our house. Someone had told them about us, that there were kidnapped girls held hostage there. Miriam was not there at that time. The soldiers asked us if a Boko Haram woman was tending to us. I was the only one who answered. I said, "Yes." "When you see her, let us know," the soldiers said.

A little bit later, Miriam returned to cook for us. She didn't suspect anything. I had secretly sent the boy off to the soldiers. Soon, they were outside the house in two pickups. Miriam saw them from the kitchen. She quickly removed her veil so she would look like a Christian. The soldiers entered and asked, "Where is the woman?" We were quiet. When they asked a second time, I pointed at Miriam. "Zainab!" she cried. "How can you be so cruel!" The soldiers pummeled her in the face with their fists and dragged her out of the house. They threw her onto the flatbed of a pickup truck. The whole time she cursed me. "You miserable girls! After everything I did for you! I cooked for you! I protected you!"

I saw her one last time. She was in the prison wing of the barracks, behind bars. The soldiers brought me there to question me. Miriam wept and hid her head in her lap. "What sort of punishment should we give you?" the soldiers asked her. I told them everything she had done to us. As I was leaving, a soldier told Miriam, "You will die of hunger. We will let you starve to death here." That is the last time I saw her. I have no idea what happened to her.

To push Boko Haram out of the cities it had conquered, the fighting power of four armies was needed. Troops from Chad, Niger, and Cameroon came to Nigeria's assistance. Nigeria itself hired hundreds of mercenaries from South Africa and Israel. The United States, which up to that point had only haltingly supported Nigeria's military, accompanied the attack with drones sent from Chad over the state of Borno. One city after another fell to the alliance. Still, at the edge of the Sambisa and off the A13, its march came to a standstill.

**Lydia:** A few days later, I was taken to a hospital in Yola. My thighbone had set the wrong way and was now crooked. So one of the priests took me to see Maidari, a bone setter. This man broke my leg a second time. Without anesthetic. Later, X-rays showed that one leg bone had set normally, but not the other one. So I had to return to Maidari, and he broke my leg once again. I now very much hope that they heal properly. The pain is so terrible every time he breaks my legs. I am so afraid now.

My mother was also able to flee to Yola with two of her children. She has now married for the third time. She met this new husband in a refugee camp. He's a driver. He already has two wives, even though he's a Christian. He helped us a lot. I have no contact with my mother anymore. Lucky also came to Yola. He joined himself to the great stream of refugees. He lived all those weeks with other families in the hills.

Grandma made it to Abuja. She made it out of the house that had been hit by the bomb. From there, she ran to the bush. In one village, she asked a man with a moped to drive her to Yola. There, she went to the bank, withdrew everything she had, and took the bus to Abuja, where her three sons live. Only three days ago did she return to Mubi. She wants to get the restaurant up and running again.

The waitresses went to Michika. They don't want to work for Grandma anymore. The girls searched for me the whole time I was a hostage, but Grandma did not. She didn't give a damn what happened to us. The waitresses now work the fields in Michika. I've heard that Grandma has new girls working for her. She still hasn't tried to get in touch with me. She is very hard-hearted.

I want to go to school again. I want to study medicine and be a doctor.

She laughs, embarrassed.

**Lydia:** I don't know. I am so confused. I just live one day at a time.

Clara, 16, a student in the ninth grade, was raised by her aunt. Members of Boko Haram kept her hostage in a camp for abducted women. She cannot remember how long she was there.

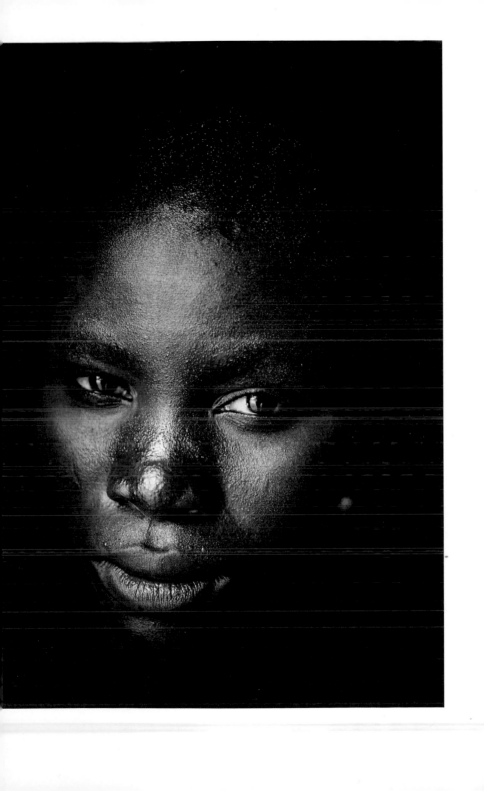

Previous two pages: Zarahu, 41, a market woman, was held hostage for a week. Of her eight children, four are still missing.

Lydia, 17, a student in the ninth grade, was held hostage for a month. During a battle, both her legs and an arm were shattered.

Mairo, 24, a friend of Clara, a farmer, and a mother of three who was a hostage for seven months.

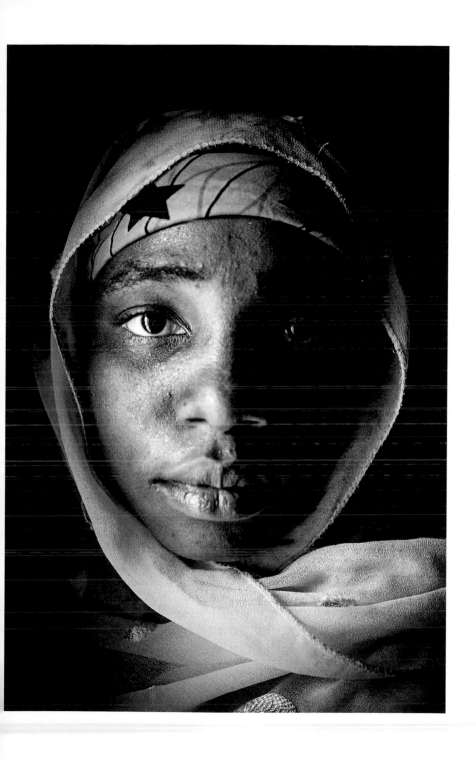

Jara, 16, a student in the eighth grade, was taken for six months and forced to marry. Her son, Ahmed, is named after her abuser.

Agnes, 25, is a market woman and Sakinah's half sister. She was held for a year in the Sambisa and forced to marry.

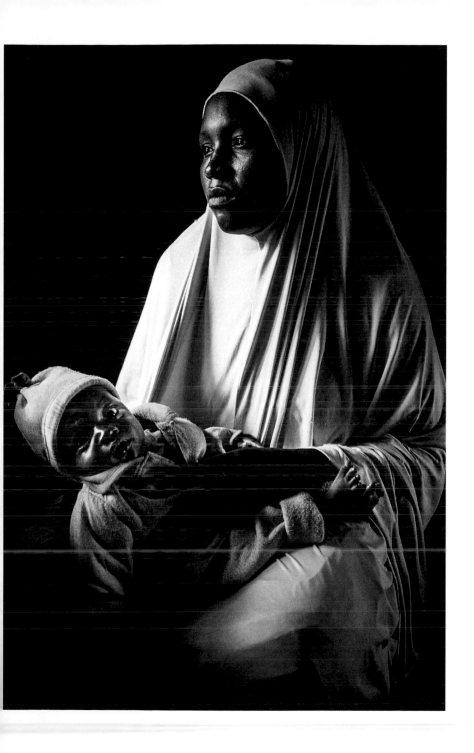

Salamatu, 38 and mother of five children, grows corn and beans in her village. Boko Haram held her for three months, during which time she was forced to marry.

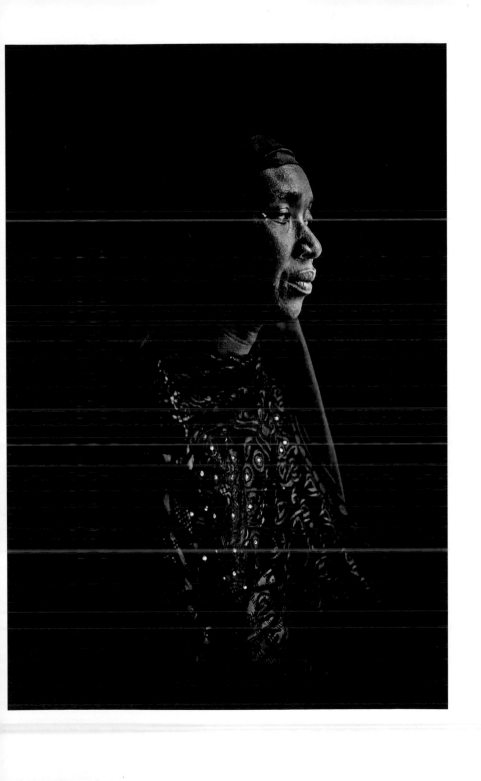

Previous two pages: Together again—January 2016. Through donations a few women have at least the material goods they need to survive.

"These people [Boko Haram] have a certain spiritual conviction that any child they father will grow to inherit their ideology, whether they live with the child or not. They also believe that whoever does not hold their ideology is an unbeliever who should be killed and rendered homeless and whatever belongs to him or her becomes a legitimate booty recovered from enemies. This booty includes women who are then allocated to ranking leaders of the sect as sex slaves. The sect leaders make very conscious effort to impregnate the women. Some of them, I was told, even pray before mating, offering supplications for God to make the products of what they are doing become children who will inherit their ideology."

—*Kashim Shettima, governor of Borno State, in an interview, May 2015*

# THE CHILD

The rain has finally started to fall, but only lightly. The roads to the north are still passable. Agnes made it to Yola yesterday. She is the last of the women with whom we speak. She is the half sister of Sakinah, the midwife. Sakinah also comes to the interview. We choose once again to have the meeting in the garden house. The same two geckos are still there. A year ago, Boko Haram kidnapped Agnes from her village near Gulak. The twenty-five-year-old had worked in the market selling palm oil and sugar before her abduction. She is a Christian but during her captivity was forced to convert to Islam. She now wears a brown hijab. Her feet are bloody and swollen. Her lower abdomen has been hurting ever since she gave birth three months ago.

Just a few days before this interview, she fled the Sambisa. She has a fever and, sometimes, cramps. She may have an infection. This interview is very short, for we realize as we speak with her that she is in urgent need of medical care.

She has four children. A newborn boy lies on her lap. She avoids looking at him. His name is Moussa. He has large eyes that fix on everything he sees.

**Agnes:** I fled from the camp with fifty other women, but made it only to a village on the savannah because I went into labor. A family there took care of me. They helped me with the baby. It was very painful, giving birth to the baby that the man made inside me.

But I had no choice. I had to marry him there in the forest. They killed the women who refused. I saw it happen. Already in the first week that they had kidnapped me. In the last city before the forest—Gwoza—they took us to the yard of a slaughterhouse. In front of us were fifty women lying in five rows. They were tied up, hands behind their backs. Then the fighters brought in other women, the Boko Haram wives. They wore black burkas. "Behold the way women kill women!" called out an emir. Behind every one of the prisoners stepped a woman in a burka.

One of the bound women screamed that she was sorry, that she would give herself in marriage. She was untied and taken outside. So then there were only forty-nine women lying there. They counted them very carefully. We were watching from about one hundred meters away. They did not want us to come any closer in case we recognized someone and called out her name. A man gave a speech, but I did not understand. Then, this person gave the command to kill the women.

The men showed the burka-clad women how best to wield their knives. I remember seeing a man lean down to one of the victims, pressing her head down and placing the blade on the nape of her neck. One of the Boko Haram women wanted to start cutting at the throat so the captive would die quicker, but the emir forbade her. The women in burkas had to cut from the nape through to the throat.

The hostages on the floor writhed and moaned heavily. It took ten minutes for the women to cut off all the heads. The bodies twitched for a long time afterward.

I lost my real husband when Boko Haram attacked my village. They shot him. I found his body and buried it in my village. He was Christian but had four wives. He was Muslim for a while, and then became Christian again. He often changed his religion. I was married to him for nine years and have three children with him. He was not an especially good man, but not that bad, either. The children are now eight, four, and three years old.

The child that the Boko Haram fighter forced me to bear in the forest is three months old. A man who helped deliver the baby was named Moussa, so he told me to name the baby Moussa. So I did. I don't care. It's a name like any other. Let him be Moussa.

I don't love this child. I know that his father is a criminal and that the child is innocent. After giving birth, I did not want to give him milk, but the villagers said, "Take care of that child. Don't sin against God."

But what sort of person is it going to become? Even my other children know that its father belongs to the men who killed their father, my husband. This baby cries much more than my other children did when they were young. I look at it a lot and think I have to feel something for it. But I feel nothing. I should have killed it.

The women who make it out of the forest are in almost all cases left without assistance or psychological support. They escape their abductors, return to their villages, and refrain from making contact with the authorities. They are aware of how much they are mistrusted. Suspicion flourishes even between members of the same family—between those who were abducted and those who had the fortune to run away in time. The military transports individual groups of kidnapped women to the South and interns them in so-called deradicalization camps. There, even close family members are not allowed to visit the women. We've been told they are interrogated, threatened, and even beaten. These women are still not free, not by any stretch. Only their jailers have changed.

Every week during its raids, Boko Haram abducts more girls and women. This book stops, but it does not end. For right now, at this moment these stories are repeating themselves all over again, somewhere in a small village not yet marked on any map.

In the hills between Gulak and Gubla there is a split in the rock, and no one knows how deep it goes. The ground abruptly opens up to a black abyss. The opening of this pit is not particularly large; it's said an adult cow would just fit through. It is so deep that the darkness eats any light beamed into it. If you throw a stone in to sound its depths, it will be lost in silence. In earlier times, people would sit at the lip and look down for the terrifying thrill of it. Residents of nearby villages now say that Boko Haram fighters were the first to throw corpses down this barathrum. Only in recent months, however, have citizen militias turned it into a mass grave. Villagers often see pickups laden with corpses driving out to the hole. How many bodies have been tossed down is not known. In December 2015, militias in Gulak reportedly shot twenty members of a family clan and then brought the bodies to the hole. Some said they were killed because they cooperated with Boko Haram. In fact, the killings were due to a feud between two extended families. For villagers nearby, approaching this hole is considered very dangerous because it is often patrolled by soldiers or members of the militias. Throughout the region, people speak of this split in the rocks. It is the place where everything comes to an end. They call it simply "the maw."

# EPILOGUE

When I return from my trips abroad, I am often asked, "What's that got to do with us?" In the West we don't like to occupy ourselves with suffering—the suffering of others. "What's the point?" I am asked in an accusatory tone. "Why do we have to care about this? Does it change anything just because we know about it?"

It changes everything.

These days, no madness that flares up in another country stays within the borders of that country. We thought for a long time we could turn away from the killings in Syria. What do problems in Syria have to do with us? Decisions made in Damascus are now of greater consequence for the local politicians in the capitals in Germany or the USA.

We cannot hide any longer. The world has become smaller. This truism from the logistics sector is one whose full meaning we still have not grasped. Shoes from Scotland, ordered and paid for, reach any address in Germany within two days. The flipside of this phenomenon is that the shock waves of distant bombs also reach us in an ever-shorter time span.

Many cannot pinpoint Nigeria on a map. Many have no connection to this country. It has produced no Hollywood actor we recognize, no sports star whose name we know, no brand name product that we use every day apart from oil. Nigeria had the Biafran War; the Niger River delta is contaminated by oil—even people interested in world politics don't know much more than that. We in the West do not look outside ourselves. We look inside, deep into our hearts, which we continually try to fathom and understand. But globalization has done away with the exterior. Many of us still do not understand this. Or we are too afraid to understand it. In the past few decades the interior has merged with the exterior.

Just over the narrow middle sea from Europe is Africa, an entire continent going through seismic change. Many African countries are falling to ruin. In the past few years, I have toured the rubble: Libya, divided into three parts now; Mali, whose northern reaches were almost turned into an Islamic state; Niger, which is threatening to fall to pieces; and Chad, whose capital city is surrounded by a gigantic antitank ditch to prevent rebels from attacking and taking the city.

If political structures finally collapse, and if no viable alternative to them is found, chaos will ensue, and various radicalized factions will clash in an attempt to create a new order and balance. The shock waves will quickly reach Europe and the Western world.

There are no easy solutions. For this reason, we need to look closely, much more closely than we have been, at what is happening in Nigeria. Economic assistance often peters out in state coffers and promotes only corruption. Military aid frequently leads only to more massacres and human rights abuses. Military solutions alone will not pacify the region, even if Boko Haram is hobbled for a while. Violence has so far made Boko Haram only stronger. Nongovernmental organizations find it almost impossible to carry out their work because they immediately become targets of attack and abduction. The worst solution, however, would be to look away, to give up, to yield to the gravity of helplessness.

It is not easy to provide help to the people of north Nigeria. Villages that openly accept assistance from aid organizations are often attacked and plundered by Boko Haram. The gift of money can quickly become poison. Once the *Zeit-Magazin*, the magazine supplement of Germany's *Die Zeit* newspaper, published portions of this book, we called on readers to donate money. Christians and Muslims whom we trusted worked for weeks in compiling a list of 151 girls and women, all of whom had been Boko Haram captives. After escaping, they had all returned to the villages from which they had been abducted, returning as well to the same risks and vulnerabilities.

As before, these girls and women, whose stories are collected here, still run from their houses in fear and spend nights in the fields where they feel safer.

After much consultation, we decided to set up bank accounts for the former hostages. They can withdraw only a small sum every month. We hope this prevents any further kidnappings. Most of the women want to buy seed and fertilizer. Many have opened market stands with the money. All want to send their children to school because they can now afford the fees. Despite everything, there is no guarantee that this money will not bring calamity down on them. The fight against Boko Haram is far from over.

We have fear. We have hope.

# ACKNOWLEDGMENTS

I thank all those who helped to make this book possible, above all those whom I cannot name without endangering their lives. Without them—those who made contact with the women I interviewed, those who translated, those who protected us—this book would not have been possible. I thank my wonderful colleague at Die Zeit Sabine Rückert, who provided the impetus for this project. I am grateful to the photographer Andy Spyra for his passion, which he shared with me, and to the team at the American University of Nigeria for its logistical help. I thank Father Maurice Kwairanga from Bistum Yola who made many things easier for us. I also wish to thank fellow reporter Kabir Anwar for his immeasurable patience and his deep humanity; my colleagues at Die Zeit, Jörg Burger, Dr. Ulrich Stolte, the still-unrecognized author of fantasy novels, and Christine Keck, for reviewing the manuscript and for a few other things, as well.

Finally, I thank the women. I thank them for their patience and the trust they gave us. I thank them for the strength they gave me. They are very strong.

# BIBLIOGRAPHICAL NOTE

*In the course of writing and researching this book I consulted two valuable books on Boko Haram: Boko Haram: Nigeria's Islamist Insurgency by Virginia Comolli and Boko Haram: Inside Nigeria's Unholy War by Mike Smith.*

*I also consulted the following reports and articles:*

"Boko Haram: Islamism, Politics, Security and the State in Nigeria," edited by Marc-Antoine Pérouse de Montclos, African Studies Centre (ASC) Institut Français de Recherche en Afrique (IFRA), West African Politics and Society Series, vol. 2, https://openaccess.leidenuniv.nl/bitstream/handle/1887/23853/ASC-075287668-3441-01.pdf

"Curbing Violence in Nigeria (II): The Boko Haram Insurgency" (Africa Report N°216), International Crisis Group, http://www.crisisgroup.org/~/media/Files/africa/west-africa/nigeria/216-curbing-violence-in-nigeria-ii-the-boko-haram-insurgency.pdf

"Cameroon and Boko Haram: Time to Think beyond Terrorism and Security," Denis M. Tull, Stiftung Wissenschaft und Politik (German Institute for International and Security Affairs), https://www.swp-berlin.org/fileadmin/contents/products/comments/2015C42_tll.pdf

"'Any child they father will grow to inherit their ideology' . . . " Njadvara Musa, *The Guardian*, http://guardian.ng/news/any-child-they-father-will-grow-to-inherit-their-ideology/

"Leadership Analysis of Boko Haram and Ansaru in Nigeria," Jacob Zenn, *CTC Sentinel*, https://www.ctc.usma.edu/posts/leadership-analysis-of-boko-haram-and-ansaru-in-nigeria

"Markets," from *The Mandara Margi: A Society Living on the Verge*, James H. Vaughan, http://www.indiana.edu/~margi/page8.shtml

"How Northern Nigeria's Violent History Explains Boko Haram," John Neville Hare, *National Geographic*, http://news.nationalgeographic.com/2015/03/150314-boko-haram-nigeria-borno-rabih-abubakar-shekau/

"Spiraling Violence: Boko Haram Attacks and Security Force Abuses in Nigeria," Human Rights Watch, https://www.hrw.org/report/2012/10/11/spiraling-violence/boko-haram-attacks-and-security-force-abuses-nigeria

"Sufism in Northern Nigeria: Force for Counter-Radicalization?," Jonathan N.C. Hill, Strategic Studies Institute, http://www.strategicstudiesinstitute.army.mil /pdffiles/pub989.pdf

"The Etymology of Hausa boko," Paul Newman, Mega-Chad Research Network, http://www.megatchad.net/publications/Newman-2013-Etymology-of-Hausa -boko.pdf

"Boko Haram Movement in Nigeria: Beginnings, Principles and Activities," Ahmad Murtada, http://download.salafimanhaj.com/pdf/SalafiManhaj _BokoHaram.pdf

# NOTES

## The Forest

1. "Africa's New Number One: Nigeria's suddenly supersized economy is indeed a wonder; but so are its still-huge problems," *The Economist*, April 12, 2014, www.economist.com/news/leaders/21600685-nigerias-suddenly-supersized -economy-indeed-wonder-so-are-its-still-huge

2. "Spiraling Violence: Boko Haram Attacks and Security Force Abuses in Nigeria," Human Rights Watch, October 11, 2012, https://www.hrw.org/report /2012/10/11/spiraling-violence/boko-haram-attacks-and-security-force-abuses -nigeria

3. Data on the levels of literacy in Nigeria can be found in a UNESCO Action Plan: "High-level International Round Table on Literacy: Reaching the 2015 Literacy Target: Delivering on the Promise," UNESCO, Paris, September 6–7, 2012, www.unesco.org/new/fileadmin/MULTIMEDIA/HQ/ED/pdf/Nigeria.pdf

4. UN Data on Life Expectancy: http://data.un.org/Data.aspx?d=WDI&f=Indi cator_Code%3ASP.DYN.LE00.IN

5. "Nigerians Living in Poverty Rise to Nearly 61%," *BBC News*, February 13, 2012, www.bbc.com/news/world-africa-17015873

6. "Curbing Violence in Nigeria (II): The Boko Haram Insurgency," International Crisis Group Africa Report N°216, April 3, 2014, www.crisisgroup.org /~/media/Files/africa/west-africa/nigeria/216-curbing-violence-in-nigeria-ii-the -boko-haram-insurgency.pdf

7. Ibid.

## The Tree

1. United Nations Office on Drugs and Crime, "Nigeria's Corruption Busters," www.unodc.org/unodc/en/frontpage/nigerias-corruption-busters.html

## ABOUT THE AUTHOR

**Wolfgang Bauer** works for the leading weekly German newspaper *Die Zeit*. For his reportage he won the Katholischer Medienpreis (Catholic Media Prize) and the Prix Bayeux-Calvados des Correspondants de Guerre. He is the author of *Stolen Girls* (The New Press) and lives in Berlin.

## ABOUT THE TRANSLATOR

**Eric Trump** is a writer and translator who teaches German studies and medical ethics at Vassar College.